ONE-DISH MEALS

Catherine Pagano Fulde

BRISTOL PUBLISHING ENTERPRISES
San Leandro, California

a nitty gritty® cookbook

Cover design: Frank J. Paredes
Cover photography: John A. Benson
Food styling: Susan Massey
Illustrations: Shanti Nelson

Printed in the United States of America.

ISBN: 1-55867-222-2

CONTENTS

ONE-DISH MEALS: TIME SAVED IN A POT

One-dish meals have achieved longevity for reasons of convenience and necessity. Many of our classical slow-cooked meals have historical roots. Labor-intensive lifestyles made time a precious commodity. Families spent long hours working and daily nourishment came from the stew pot, which was started early in the day. Slow cooking also worked to make food palatable; ingenious cooks used fragrant herbs and aromatic spices to create culinary treasures.

Lifestyles today, although much more sophisticated, still suffer from the same complication – they leave little time for elaborate meal preparation. Working families looking for alternatives to restaurant dining and precooked meals are turning back to time-efficient home cooking. Wholesome meals can be prepared ahead of time, as in days of old, or quickly at dinner time, utilizing technological advances.

The food processor reduces preparation time; the microwave oven shortens cooking times and simplifies cooking methods; the freezer brings cooked or partially cooked foods to our fingertips. One-dish meals combine proteins, grains, vegetables, fruits, spices, herbs, liquids and ingenuity with modern methods and technology. The recipes in this book provide the answer to easy, delicious, healthful dining. They focus on ease of preparation for both daily dining (breakfast, lunch and dinner) and company fare. Dishes include both classical and contemporary entrees that fit into modern lifestyles.

In addition to considering food types (meats, chicken, fish, vegetables) and methods (baked, broiled, sautéed, stir-fried), attention is paid to healthful aspects. Wherever possible, herbs, seasonings and defatted broths reduce cooking fat and replace gravies; nonfat, low-fat, and low-sodium products are used, reflecting the interest in healthful eating without sacrificing richness of flavor.

With just one pot to prepare and only a few pans to wash, precious time can be spent on activities of your choice.

ABOUT THE RECIPES

One-dish cooking need not be restricted to cold-weather comfort meals. These recipes introduce to your table the fresh foods of spring, the easy-living meals of summer and the mellow-rich tastes of autumn, as well as the hearty dishes of winter.

Cooking with the bounty of the seasons reflects a lighter approach to food preparation. Classics like spinach salad with bacon and boeuf bourguignon are transformed into a *Spinach Salad with Porcini and Pine Nuts*, page 16, and a *California Beef Burgundy*, page 34, seasoned with an abundance of fresh marjoram and Burgundy wine. Special care has been taken to showcase family and company dinners. One-dish meals such as *Vegetable Curry*, page 46, *Sizzling Tortilla Soup*, page 68, and *Beef Wraps with Spicy Salsa*, page 84, will keep your family satisfied and save you time. *Impromptu Shrimp Alfredo,* page 52, saves the day (provided you have the fixings in the freezer and pantry) when unexpected dinner guests appear. There is also an abundance of quick meals that take 30 minutes or less to prepare. Try *Crunchy Vegetable Burritos*, page 147, *Garden Pea Shoot Salad*, page 132, or *Sea Bass with Citrus*, page 164. You will find cooking is enjoyable when preparations are kept to the bare minimum.

ABOUT THE INGREDIENTS

Throwing ingredients into a pot and cooking them is not going to produce a great-tasting meal. Time is wasted if the food is tasteless. Sautéing garlic and onions is necessary to give a dish flavor. Browning meats with spices and herbs before baking in a casserole also adds flavor. The eventual success is worth the extra effort. When looking at these recipes, do not be intimidated by the list of ingredients – realize that many of them are spices and herbs. Reduced-fat and low-salt cooking relies on these additional flavors to perk up the taste.

"You can't make a silk purse out of a sow's ear!" This old folk expression carries over into the kitchen. Soups, stews, casseroles and sandwiches will be only as good as the ingredients that go into them. Always use the best quality and freshest food that is available. Home-grown vegetables and herbs obviously are the best. Don't be tempted to "clean out the refrigerator" when making soup. Tired vegetables belong in the compost heap; old leftovers in the trash bin. Success with these recipes will depend on the use of fresh, high-quality ingredients. Extra virgin olive oil is the preferred oil in most of the recipes. It is more economical to buy one grade of olive oil to use for cooking and for dressing than to have several open bottles of various grades, since olive oil does not improve with age. Extra virgin is the least refined of the olive oils and, therefore, the most natural. Select a brand that suits your taste.

If you are fond of cooking ethnic recipes and insist on authenticity, however, you may consider investing in small bottles of extra virgin olive oil pressed from native olives. Likewise, when you choose wine, pick up a bottle that reflects the origin of the dish. A spicy California white could make a pleasing companion to a light and fresh meal prepared with West Coast ingredients, or a juicy Italian red might well accompany a number of pasta dishes. Not only is wine and food more enjoyable when thought about in this manner, but this pairing allows one to taste the individual ingredients.

Flavored oils are a good investment in time, taste and value. Porcini mushroom and white truffle oils add a luxurious touch to home-cooked entrées without the cost or labor-intense preparation of the fresh commodity. Look for the smallest possible bottles since shelf life is not long. Herb-infused oils and vinegars also impart flavor while saving preparation time.

Nonfat condensed milk can be enriched with nonfat powdered milk so that it takes on some of the properties of light cream without the fat. Whisk the nonfat powdered milk into the condensed milk until thick and creamy. Use it as the base for creamed soups, white sauces and Alfredo sauce, and as thickening for pan drippings.

Most of us today do not have the time or the discipline to set a day aside each week to prepare beef, chicken, vegetable and fish stocks to enhance our food preparation. Fortunately, canned, frozen and condensed dried broths are widely available in the market. When selecting canned broths, look for low-sodium varieties, and remove any visible fat before using. Frozen condensed broths, although considerably more expensive than canned, are high-quality products without excessive salt, but are not widely available. Concentrated dry stocks come in both cubes and powders. Once again, they tend to be salty, but when enough liquid is used, they are satisfactory. Demi-glace, a rich brown reduction sauce, is available in solid form. It is more complex, richer and, of course, higher in calories than soup stocks, but a tiny bit adds "simmered all day" flavor to quickly prepared soups and stews.

Specific ethnic ingredients are listed for use in cultural dishes. Use them to capture the taste of the cuisine. Fortunately, markets today, aware of consumer preferences, stock these items in special ethnic food sections.

TIME SAVING TIPS

Preparation time can be greatly reduced by implementing some of the following strategies:

- Organize your pantry, refrigerator and freezer so similar foods are always stored on the same shelf and are easy to find.
- Read the recipe several times for clarity and assemble all ingredients before beginning to cook.
- Use the food processor whenever recipes require many vegetables to be chopped, shredded or sliced. The time saved is more than the time taken to clean the appliance.
- To shorten preparation time, buy frozen vegetables that are prechopped, sliced and blanched. There is an assortment of vegetables that rival fresh ones. Onions are available chopped, sliced and whole in the freezer section. Fresh garlic can be purchased minced, chopped or peeled. Both are available in powder and freeze-dried forms. Jars of peeled and chopped fresh ginger are available in the produce section. Bagged, undressed, premixed salad assortments are found in the produce sections of most markets.
- Line shallow baking pans with foil before cooking to save cleanup time.

- Use knives that are sharp. Food cuts easily with fewer accidents. A dull knife only saws food and will cause undesirable-looking cuts and frustration.
- Plan ahead so that extra portions are prepared the night before. Some recipes lend themselves to partial preparation. Precooked foods are time savers. Roast an extra chicken when preparing a chicken dinner, cook extra rice for the next day's dinner or buy prepared foods from the neighborhood deli or rotisserie. With marinated foods, mix the ingredients well, cover and refrigerate overnight. The next day, bring to room temperature before continuing with the recipe. Wash and spin-dry packaged, loose and head salad greens. Romaine, endive and escarole can be torn into bite-size pieces before storing between paper towels in a plastic bag.
- A rice cooker is a wonderful way to prepare fresh rice for a recipe, resulting in no-worry, perfect-tasting rice. A microwave oven saves valuable minutes. Use this indispensable appliance whenever possible. Cooking polenta and risotto in the microwave takes minutes and requires little stirring.
- Freeze, using only moisture- and vapor-proof freezer bags.

CLASSICS WITH A TWIST

CREAMY CARROT SOUP

Servings: 6

This soup hints of Asia with sesame oil and spices. An herb-flavored bread is well-suited to this nourishing, warm soup.

¼ cup unsalted butter
2 tbs. sesame oil
1 large yellow onion, sliced
2 leeks (white part only), washed and sliced
5 cloves garlic, chopped
½ cup chopped fresh ginger
8 cups low-sodium chicken broth
2 cups dry white wine
2 lb. carrots, peeled and sliced
1 tsp. curry powder
¼ tsp. cinnamon
¼ tsp. nutmeg
salt and white pepper to taste
chopped fresh chives for garnish

In a large stockpot over medium-high heat, melt butter. Add sesame oil, onion, leeks, garlic and ginger. Bring to a boil. Lower heat to medium and cook, stirring frequently, for 20 minutes, until onion and leeks are soft and transparent. Add chicken broth, wine and carrots. Cover and bring to a boil. Lower heat to medium and simmer for 40 minutes, until carrots are soft. Remove from heat and cool. Transfer to the workbowl of a food processor or blender container and process until smooth. Add curry, cinnamon, nutmeg, salt and pepper. When ready to serve, reheat soup and garnish with chives.

SMOKED TURKEY AND SPLIT PEA SOUP

Servings: 4-6

Using smoked turkey rather than ham reduces fat without parting with flavor. Caraway-seeded bread, unsalted butter and applesauce complete the dinner.

2 cups split peas, washed and picked over
4 qt. cold water
2 tbs. canola oil
4 large smoked turkey legs
1 onion, chopped
2 carrots, peeled and coarsely chopped
2 stalks celery, coarsely chopped
2 qt. cold water
1 large bay leaf
1 cup fresh mixed herb leaves (marjoram, thyme, parsley), tightly packed
salt and pepper to taste
1/4 lb. turkey franks, cooked and cut into 1-inch slices

In a stockpot, bring peas and water to a boil. Remove from heat, cover and soak for 15 minutes. Drain peas and set aside. In same stockpot over medium heat, heat oil. Cook turkey, onion, carrots and celery for 5 minutes, or until lightly brown. Add water, stirring to release browned bits on bottom of pot. Add peas, herbs, salt and pepper. Cover and simmer for 1 hour. Remove meat from turkey bones, and discard bones. Return meat to pot. Place mixture in a food processor workbowl or blender container and process until just mixed. Stir in turkey frank slices. Taste and adjust seasonings.

SHREDDED BEET SOUP WITH FINNISH FLATBREAD

Servings: 6

The classic Russian borscht acquires a Finnish accent with the flavors of red cabbage and carrots. Orange juice, orange zest, brown rice and green onion-spiked sour cream adds a Yankee touch. The Karelian Finns serve their beet soup with Rieska, a multigrain flatbread.

4 medium beets, peeled and shredded
2 tbs. butter
1 tsp. salt
1/4 cup flour
2 tsp. cider vinegar
2 tbs. orange juice
1 small head red cabbage, shredded
1 bay leaf
2 cloves garlic, mashed
2 carrots, peeled and sliced
1 tbs. sugar
1 tsp. grated fresh orange peel (zest)
8 cups beef or vegetable broth
1 1/2 cups sour cream
4 green onions, finely chopped
2 cups cooked brown rice
1 lemon, thinly sliced

In a large stockpot over medium heat, brown shredded beets in butter until limp. Add salt, flour, vinegar and orange juice. Mix until all lumps are dissolved and mixture is well blended. Add cabbage, bay leaf, garlic, carrots, sugar, zest and broth. Bring to a boil. Lower heat to medium and simmer for at least 2 hours, or until vegetables are soft. Remove bay leaf. Just before serving, mix sour cream with green onions. Heat rice and place in warm bowls. Ladle in soup and top with a dollop of sour cream mixture. Pass lemon slices.

ARMENIAN SHISH KEBABS WITH RICE

Servings: 4

Outdoor shish kebabs are brought indoors with this oven-baked dinner. Marinated lamb and lots of vegetables bake on top of hot, seasoned rice.

2 tbs. extra virgin olive oil
1/4 cup dry red wine
1 medium onion, chopped
2 tbs. minced garlic
2 tsp. minced fresh ginger
1 1/2 tsp. ground allspice
salt and pepper to taste
1 1/2 lb. boneless lamb shoulder, cut into 2 1/2-inch cubes
8 medium white mushrooms, stems chopped and caps left whole
1 cup uncooked rice
3 cups beef or vegetable broth, defatted
8 large cherry tomatoes
1 pkg. (10 oz.) frozen small onions, thawed
2 medium-sized green bell peppers, stemmed,
seeded and cut into 2 1/2-inch squares

In a locking plastic storage bag, combine olive oil, wine, onion, 1½ tbs. of the garlic, 1½ tsp. of the ginger, 1 tsp. of the allspice, salt, pepper and lamb. Mix well and refrigerate for 3 to 6 hours, turning bag occasionally.

Heat oven to 350°. In a shallow 2-quart casserole, combine remaining ½ tbs. garlic, ½ tsp. ginger, ½ tsp. allspice, mushroom stems, rice and broth; mix well. Remove lamb from marinade and arrange on 4 skewers, alternating with mushroom caps, tomatoes, onions and peppers. Brush kabobs with marinade and arrange on rice mixture. Bake until kabobs are tender and rice is cooked, about 1¼ hours. Do not overcook. Check for doneness after 1 hour.

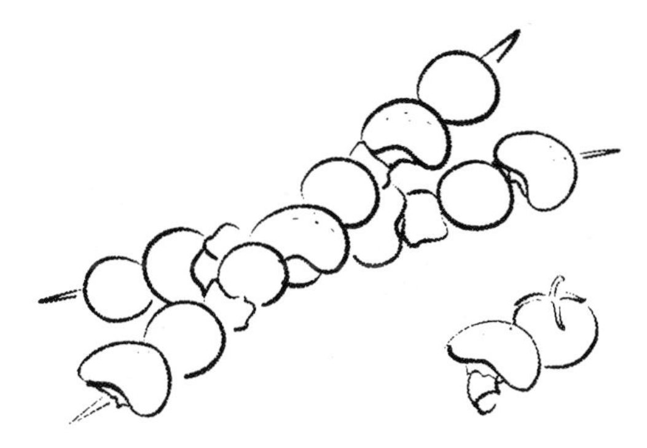

SPINACH SALAD WITH PORCINI MUSHROOMS AND PINE NUTS

Servings: 4

Sometimes a light supper is most satisfying on a warm evening. Use pancetta, Italy's salt- and spice-cured bacon, instead of domestic smoke-cured bacon.

4 oz. dried porcini mushrooms
1 cup boiling water
¼ cup extra virgin olive oil
¼ lb. pancetta, diced
2 large bunches spinach, or 8 cups baby spinach leaves, washed and dried
¼ cup balsamic vinegar
1 cup toasted pine nuts
4 hard-cooked eggs, thinly sliced

Soak mushrooms for 20 minutes in boiling water. In a skillet over medium-high heat, heat 2 tbs. olive oil and sauté pancetta for 15 minutes, until brown and crisp; remove and set aside. Drain mushrooms in a sieve and squeeze mushrooms under running water to remove any remaining grit. Dry, slice and add to pan drippings. Sauté for 4 minutes, until cooked. Add remaining 2 tbs. olive oil and vinegar to skillet. Fold in spinach and pancetta, mixing well. Arrange on plates and top with pine nuts and egg slices.

LINGUINI WITH CLAMS

Servings: 2-3

Chopped clams, extra virgin olive oil, garlic, celery and a few herbs produce a quick lunch or light dinner in the time it takes to cook the linguini. Try this easy entrée the next time you are in a rush. For a nontraditional layer of flavor, sprinkle with cheese and drizzle with extra olive oil.

½ lb. fresh or dried linguini
¼ cup extra virgin olive oil
3 cloves garlic, minced
¼ tsp. red pepper flakes
1½ cups chopped celery
3 tbs. chopped fresh oregano
2 cans (6.5 oz. each) chopped clams, drained, juice reserved
1 cup chopped fresh flat-leaf parsley
extra virgin olive oil
grated pecorino Romano cheese

In a large skillet, cook olive oil, garlic and red pepper over medium heat until garlic is fragrant, but not browned. Add celery, oregano and clam juice, reserving clams. Cover and cook for about 4 minutes, until celery is tender-crisp. Stir in clams and parsley.

Cook linguini in a large pot of rapidly boiling salted water until slightly firm to the bite, *al dente*, about 3 minutes. Drain pasta, leaving a little water clinging to it, and place in a warm bowl. Spoon red pepper mixture and clams over pasta. Mix lightly and spoon onto dinner plates, passing the extra virgin olive oil and cheese.

PENNETTE PASTA WITH MUSHROOMS

Servings: 4

In this unusual dish, dried pasta is prepared as if it were risotto.

3 tbs. extra virgin olive oil
½ lb. cremini (brown) mushrooms, sliced
2 cloves garlic, minced
3 tbs. chopped fresh flat-leaf parsley
pinch red pepper flakes
1 lb. pennette pasta
¼ cup dry sherry
3½ cups beef broth, defatted
1 cup half-and-half
1 cup grated Parmesan cheese
salt and pepper to taste

In a large nonstick skillet, heat 2 tbs. of the olive oil over medium heat. Add mushrooms, garlic, 2 tbs. of the parsley and red pepper flakes and cook, stirring constantly for 2 minutes, until mushrooms are tender; set aside. Add remaining 1 tbs. oil to skillet and increase the heat to medium-high. Add pennette and cook, stirring constantly for 4 minutes, until pasta turns a deep golden brown. Add sherry and cook until evaporated. Lower heat to medium and add enough broth to barely cover pasta. Cook for about 10 minutes, stirring frequently and adding broth as needed until pasta is tender. Stir in half-and-half. Remove from heat and stir in cheese, mushroom mixture and remaining 1 tbs. parsley. Season with salt and pepper and serve immediately.

PASTA WITH SWORDFISH

Servings: 4

A variation of the Sicilian dish pasta with sardines, this recipe substitutes swordfish.

1 lb. fresh linguini
1/2 cup raisins
2 pinches saffron threads
1 cup Marsala wine
1 cup pine nuts
4 swordfish fillets, 4 oz. each, cut into 2-inch strips
1/4 cup extra virgin olive oil
2 medium bulbs fennel, thinly sliced
1 large onion, thinly sliced
salt and pepper to taste
chopped fresh fennel leaves for garnish
1/4 cup fresh breadcrumbs, toasted

Cook linguini in a large pot of rapidly boiling salted water until slightly firm to the bite, *al dente*, about 3 minutes. Drain pasta, leaving a little water clinging to it, place in a warm bowl and set aside. Soak raisins and saffron in wine. In a large skillet over medium-high heat, toast pine nuts; set aside. In same skillet, stir-fry swordfish strips in oil in several batches for 5 minutes each, or until golden around edges. Set aside cooked fish. Combine fennel and onion and stir-fry in batches for 3 to 4 minutes each, until tender-crisp. Add pine nuts, raisins, wine and swordfish to skillet. Cook, stirring gently, until wine evaporates. Toss with pasta, garnish with fennel and pass breadcrumbs for sprinkling.

CHICKEN FRIED RICE

Servings: 4

Fried rice is a tasty meal that takes little time to prepare. For best results, cook the rice the night before, refrigerate it and separate the grains when ready to use.

3 tbs. light soy sauce
pinch red pepper flakes
1 tbs. chicken broth
1½ tbs. sake (Japanese rice wine)
1 tsp. sesame oil
5 cups cooked white rice, chilled
2½ tsp. peanut or corn oil
2 large eggs
3 carrots, peeled and cut into ¼-inch dice
2 stalks celery, cut into ¼-inch dice
1½ cups cut snow pea pieces
1 tbs. minced garlic
2 tbs. minced fresh ginger
2 cups bite-sized cooked chicken pieces
¼ cup sesame seeds, toasted

In a bowl, stir soy sauce, red pepper flakes, chicken broth, sake and sesame oil; set aside. Spread rice into a shallow pan and separate grains with a fork; set aside. In a deep 12-inch nonstick skillet, heat oil over medium-high heat and stir-fry eggs for 30 seconds, until scrambled. Add carrots, celery, snow peas, garlic and ginger. Stir-fry for 2 minutes, until vegetables are tender-crisp. Add chicken and rice. Cook for 2 to 3 minutes, or until heated through. Add soy sauce mixture, tossing to coat. Top with toasted sesame seeds and serve.

SAUSAGE AND ARTICHOKE RISOTTO

Servings: 6

The robust flavor of this risotto comes from low-fat specialty turkey sausage, artichoke hearts and a good-quality broth.

3 tbs. unsalted butter
2 tbs. vegetable oil
1 medium onion, finely chopped
2 cloves garlic, minced
1 tbs. chopped fresh sage, or 3/4 tsp. dried
1 cup finely chopped artichoke hearts (canned or frozen)
3/4 lb. smoked turkey sausage, casings removed
1 medium tomato, finely chopped
2 cups Arborio rice
1/2 cup dry white wine
5 cups good-quality beef broth
1/4 cup grated Parmesan cheese

In a heavy 2 quart saucepan, over medium-high heat, heat butter and oil and stir onion, garlic and sage until onion is translucent. Add artichoke, sausage and tomato and cook until sausage is brown. Pour in wine, stirring constantly. When wine evaporates, add rice, stirring to coat grains with butter mixture. Add 1/2 cup of broth and cook rice, stirring constantly so rice does not stick to bottom of pan. When broth is absorbed, add another 1/2 cup broth and repeat procedure. Check texture of rice after 20 minutes of cooking. Rice is finished when firm to the bite and there is no liquid left in pan. Add remaining 1 tbs. butter and cheese.

CAJUN RED BEANS AND RICE

Servings: 4

Cajun cooking is a relaxed "country-style" cooking, emphasizing simple, but spicy, flavors. Bourbon whiskey gives this dish a down-home taste and it mellows the heat of the cayenne. Serve the dish with hunks of cornbread or a simply prepared vegetable.

6 slices bacon, chopped
4 cloves garlic, minced
1 large onion, chopped
1 cup chopped celery with leaves
1 cup chopped green bell pepper
1 tsp. dried oregano, crumbled
½ lb. cooked Andouille sausage or smoked pork sausage, cut into ¾-inch pieces, casings removed
1 can (15 oz.) red beans (Louisiana-style preferred)
1 can (8 oz.) tomato sauce
2 cups instant rice
1½ cups water
¼ cup bourbon whiskey
1½ cups chopped green onions, plus more for garnish
¼ tsp. cayenne pepper

In a large skillet over medium-high heat, brown bacon. Pour off all but 2 tbs. drippings. Cook garlic, onion, celery, green pepper and oregano in skillet for 4 to 6 minutes, or until wilted. Add sausage, beans, tomato sauce, rice, water, whiskey, green onions and cayenne. Bring to a boil. Cover skillet, lower heat to simmer and cook for 10 to 12 minutes, or until rice is tender and sauce is creamy. Serve in deep dishes, garnished with green onion.

CHICKEN WITH RICE (ARROZ CON POLLO)

Servings: 6-8

Many countries have some variation of chicken with rice. The ingredients and method of preparation provide the distinction. This recipe has Spanish and Cuban roots. Saffron and ham hint at its origin and add a distinct dimension of flavor.

5 cloves garlic, minced
2 tbs. minced fresh oregano, or 2 tsp. dried
1½ tsp. salt
1½ tsp. paprika
4 lb. chicken pieces
2 tbs. extra virgin olive oil
1 medium onion, chopped
1 medium-sized green bell pepper, stemmed, seeded and chopped
1 cup diced ham
1 can (14.5 oz.) crushed tomatoes with juice
6 cups chicken broth
¼ tsp. powdered saffron
1 bay leaf
1 tbs. capers
2 cups long-grain rice
salt and pepper to taste
2 cups frozen peas
1 pkg. (8 oz.) frozen artichoke hearts
¼ cup minced roasted red bell pepper
¼ cup sharp white cheddar cheese
6 long strips roasted red bell peppers

In blender container, process garlic, oregano, salt and paprika into a paste. Loosen chicken skin and smooth paste over chicken with back of a spoon, taking care not to remove skin. Set aside for 20 minutes. Heat oven to 350°. In a large Dutch oven over medium-high heat, heat olive oil. Lightly brown chicken pieces. Transfer to bowl and set aside. In same oven, cook onion, pepper and ham for 8 to 10 minutes, or until vegetables are fragrant and ham is lightly browned. Return chicken and accumulated juices to pot with tomatoes, chicken stock, saffron, bay leaf, capers, rice, salt and pepper. Cover and bring to a boil. Remove from stove; place in oven, and bake until rice is tender, for 45 minutes. Uncover, add peas, artichoke hearts and minced peppers. Cover and continue to bake until vegetables are heated through, for 5 minutes longer. Stir in cheese and serve in bowls, garnished with roasted pepper strips.

MUSHROOM RAGOUT WITH POLENTA

Servings: 4

Porcini and shiitake mushrooms are combined in this earthy stew. Serve it on a bed of polenta, which is easily prepared in the microwave.

2 oz. dried porcini mushrooms
2 oz. dried shiitake mushrooms
2 tbs. extra virgin olive oil
1 oz. prosciutto, diced
2 cloves garlic, minced
2 cups thinly sliced yellow onion
1/4 cup chopped fresh sage
salt and pepper to taste
1/2 cup dry white wine
1/2 lb. mixed medium-sized white and brown mushrooms, cut into 1/4-inch thick slices
1/4 lb. portabello mushrooms, cut into 1/4-inch-thick slices
2 tbs. porcini oil
1/2 cup chopped fresh flat-leaf parsley
2 oz. shaved fontina cheese
polenta, follows

Soak porcini and shiitake mushrooms in cold water for 20 minutes. Drain mushrooms into a sieve, saving soaking liquid. Squeeze them under running water to remove any remaining grit. Dry, slice and set aside. Strain mushroom soaking liquid through damp paper towels and reserve. In a large skillet, heat olive oil and add prosciutto. Cook over medium-high heat, stirring constantly, until prosciutto softens. Reduce heat to medium. Add garlic, onion, sage and salt and pepper and cook for 3 minutes, or until soft.

Add wine, porcini and shiitake mushrooms, fresh mushrooms and reserved soaking liquid. Bring to a boil, reduce heat to medium and cook uncovered for 12 to 15 minutes, until liquid has reduced and mushrooms no longer release liquid. Stir in porcini oil and parsley, set aside and keep warm. Heat oven to 450° and prepare polenta.

POLENTA

Servings: 4

4 cups water
1¼ cups polenta or yellow cornmeal
2 tsp. salt
¼ cup butter
½ cups grated fontina cheese
black pepper to taste

In a 2-quart microwaveable bowl, combine water, polenta and salt. Cook on HIGH for 12 minutes, stirring once. Remove from oven and stir in butter, cheese and pepper. Pour into a 9-x-13-inch baking pan. Place mushroom ragout over polenta. Arrange shaved fontina on top. Bake on top oven rack for 5 minutes, or until cheese melts.

CHICKEN STEW MILANESE

Servings: 4

Corn muffin mix forms dumplings as it cooks atop the stew during the last 30 minutes. Use fresh, packaged chicken thighs for convenience and flavor.

1 large onion, finely chopped
1 large carrot, finely chopped
2 stalks celery, finely chopped
¼ cup butter
4 cloves garlic, minced
1 tbs. minced fresh lemon peel (zest)
¼ cup canola oil
2 lb. chicken thighs
½ cup flour
1 cup dry white wine
1½ cups chicken broth
1 can (14 oz.) chopped tomatoes with juice
2 bay leaves
2 tbs. fresh thyme leaves
½ cup chopped fresh flat-leaf parsley
salt and pepper to taste
1 pkg. (8.5 oz.) corn muffin mix
2 tbs. grated fresh lemon peel (zest)
2 cloves garlic, chopped
2 cups cooked broccoli for garnish

Heat oven to 350°. In a heavy Dutch oven, cook onion, carrot and celery in butter over medium heat for 8 minutes. Add garlic and lemon zest. Cook for 3 minutes until vegetables soften. Remove from oven and set aside. In same Dutch oven, heat oil to medium-high heat. Coat chicken with flour and quickly brown chicken in two batches. When browned, remove from pan and set aside. Drain oil and discard. Pour wine into Dutch oven. Simmer, stirring to release browned bits clinging to bottom and sides. Stir in vegetables and chicken. Add broth, tomatoes, bay leaves, thyme, 1/4 cup of the parsley, salt and pepper. Bring to a boil. Cover and bake for 20 minutes. Prepare muffin mix according to package directions, but use 3/4 cup liquid and 3 tbs. parsley. Drop spoonfuls of mix over simmering stew. Cover and bake an additional 30 minutes. Stir lemon zest, garlic and remaining 2 tbs. parsley into stew, taking care not to dislodge dumplings. Remove bay leaves and serve in large bowls over broccoli.

SWORDFISH STROGANOFF

Servings: 4

Because of its firm texture, swordfish is an ideal fish for stroganoff. Low-fat sour cream and canola oil minimize fat. Spinach fettuccine, available at specialty grocery stores, provides lovely color.

½ cup pine nuts
2 tbs. butter
¼ cup canola oil
½ lb. white mushrooms, sliced
1 large yellow onion, thinly sliced
1½ lb. swordfish, cut into ½-x-2-inch strips
salt to taste
Hungarian sweet paprika to taste, plus additional for sprinkling
1½ cups low-fat sour cream, room temperature
½ cup dry white wine
2 tsp. lemon juice
1 tsp. Worcestershire sauce
1 tsp. Dijon-style mustard
10 oz. fresh or dried spinach fettuccine
¼ cup finely chopped fresh flat-leaf parsley

Cook fettuccine according to package directions. Drain and keep warm, reserving 1/4 cup of the cooking water. In a large skillet, toast pine nuts over medium-high heat for 2 minutes, until lightly browned; set aside. In same skillet, cook mushrooms in 1/2 tbs. of the butter and 1/2 tbs. of the oil. Repeat process with onion, using another 1/2 tbs. each butter and oil.

Sprinkle swordfish pieces with salt and paprika. Sauté in two batches in remaining 1 tbs. butter and 1 tbs. oil for 5 minutes, until lightly browned. In a small bowl, whisk sour cream, wine, lemon juice, Worcestershire, mustard and reserved cooking water. Return mushrooms and onions to skillet and add sour cream mixture, stirring gently to blend. Quickly fold in warm fettuccini. Cook until mixture is hot, but not bubbling. Divide stroganoff among 4 heated plates. Sprinkle with parsley, paprika and pine nuts. Serve immediately.

TUNA PROVENÇAL

Servings: 4

Fresh tuna stars in this fragrant dish that is somewhere between a soup and a stew. The combination of herbs and citrus is country French.

¼ cup extra virgin olive oil
16 small white onions, cooked, or
 1 pkg. (10 oz.) frozen small onions
5 cloves garlic, slivered
1 medium bulb fennel, thinly sliced
4 cups diced tomatoes with juice
4 medium carrots, peeled and cut into
 1-inch chunks
1 tsp. fennel seeds
1 tsp. dried thyme leaves, crumbled
2 large bay leaves
¼ tsp. powdered saffron
1 cup dry white wine
salt and pepper to taste
1½ lb. fresh tuna fillets, cut into 1-x-2-
 inch pieces
16 brine-cured black olives, pitted
juice and grated peel (zest) of ½ orange
1 cup chopped fresh flat-leaf parsley

Heat oven to 350°. In a flameproof casserole, heat oil. Gently sauté onions, garlic and fennel for 5 minutes. Add tomatoes, carrots, fennel seeds, thyme, bay leaves, saffron, wine, salt and pepper. Simmer for 10 minutes. Stir in tuna and olives. Cover and bake for 20 minutes; uncover. Stir in orange juice, zest and parsley. Bake for 5 minutes more. Remove bay leaves before serving.

HUNGARIAN GOULASH

Servings: 4

This untraditional goulash is made with leftover roast beef, but it is seasoned traditionally with Hungarian paprika. Serve it with buttered noodles and cooked peas.

1/4 cup butter
1 tbs. canola oil
1 lb.cooked roast beef, thinly sliced
2 tsp. caraway seeds
2-4 tbs. sweet Hungarian paprika, plus more for garnish
salt and onion powder to taste
2 tbs. ketchup
1 cup beef broth
1/2 cup low-fat sour cream, optional
2 cups hot buttered noodles
1 cup cooked peas

In a saucepan over medium heat, heat butter and oil. Quickly brown beef with caraway seeds, paprika, salt and onion powder. Stir in ketchup and broth. Lower heat, cover and simmer for 20 minutes. Remove from heat and fold in sour cream, if using. Arrange noodles and peas on plates. Top with goulash and sprinkle with additional paprika.

CALIFORNIA BEEF BURGUNDY

Servings: 6-8

A variation on the classic boeuf bourguignon, this skillet supper uses Burgundy wine and an abundance of marjoram, an herb that grows wild in some areas of California. It makes a meal by itself, or serve it with a spinach salad, sourdough bread and, of course, Burgundy wine for drinking.

1 chuck roast, 3 lb.
instant meat tenderizer, optional
flour seasoned with salt, pepper and garlic powder
1/4-1/2 cup extra virgin olive oil
4 cloves garlic, minced
1 cup fresh marjoram leaves, packed
4 large carrots, peeled and cut into 1/4-inch diagonal slices
1/2 lb. white onions, peeled, or 1 pkg. (10 oz.) frozen white onions
1/2 lb. button mushrooms
2 tbs. flour
1 cup Burgundy wine
2 cups beef broth
1 1/2 cups frozen peas
4 cups hot buttered noodles

Tenderize chuck roast by following meat tenderizer package directions, if using. Cut into 2-inch pieces and coat generously with flour mixture. In a large skillet, heat 2 tbs. of the olive oil and sauté garlic. Remove cloves and discard. In same skillet, brown chuck roast pieces in three batches, adding marjoram leaves and oil as needed. Remove from skillet and set aside. Flour carrots, onions and mushrooms. Brown in batches and set aside. Sprinkle flour over drippings, stirring well until brown. Pour in wine and stock; stir constantly until thin gravy forms. Return meat and vegetables to skillet. Liquid should barely cover meat and vegetables. Bring to a boil. Lower heat and simmer, covered, for 3 hours. After 1½ hours, check liquid level. Add water, if needed. Add frozen peas 5 minutes before serving time. Serve over hot buttered noodles.

OVEN-BAKED BEEF

Servings: 6

After a long day, come home to this delicious, ready-to-serve dinner. Prepare the vegetables the night before, wrap tightly with plastic wrap and refrigerate. The following morning, prepare and bake the roast in a slow oven. Serve it with a mixed green salad and country-style bread. This cooks for 8 hours, so plan ahead!

1 blade chuck roast, 5½ lb.
8 cloves garlic, slivered
salt and pepper to taste
¼ cup herbs de Provence
¼ cup extra virgin olive oil
4 large carrots, peeled and quartered
4 large potatoes, peeled and quartered
1 large onion, cut into eighths
4 cups dry red wine
2 cups frozen peas

Heat oven to 200°. Trim all fat from roast, make 8 incisions on each side of roast and insert garlic slivers. Rub ½ of salt, pepper and herbs on top side. In an 8-½ quart Dutch oven or large, covered roasting pan, add 2 tbs. of the olive oil. Place one layer of the cut vegetables in pan. Place roast, seasoned-side down, on vegetables. Rub remaining ½ of seasoning on roast. Top with remaining vegetables. Pour wine and last 2 tbs. oil over roast; cover. Seal entire lidded pan tightly with foil. Bake for 8 hours. Stir in frozen peas 10 minutes before serving.

COMPANY FARE

OYSTER AND ARTICHOKE SOUP

Servings: 4

This creamy combination makes a great-tasting luncheon entrée which is ideal for a small group. A fruit salad and soft white rolls are suitable accompaniments.

6 shallots, thinly sliced
4 cloves garlic, minced
1/4 lb. unsalted butter
3 tbs. flour
3 cups chicken broth
2 pkg. (8 oz. each) frozen artichoke hearts, thawed and thinly sliced
2 tbs. minced fresh flat-leaf parsley
1/2 tsp. dried thyme, crumbled
1 small bay leaf
salt and white pepper to taste
2 jars (8 oz. each) small Pacific oysters with juice, cut in half

In a saucepan over medium heat, cook shallots and garlic in butter until soft. Stir in flour and cook for 3 minutes, or until golden. Remove from heat and whisk in chicken broth, mixing until smooth. Add artichokes, parsley, thyme, bay leaf and salt and pepper. Cover and simmer for 15 minutes. Add oysters and poach for 5 minutes, or until just cooked. Remove bay leaf, ladle soup into bowls and serve.

MUSHROOM QUICHE

Servings: 6

The marriage of wild and white mushrooms brings an earthy taste to this sophisticated quiche. Serve the quiche with baby salad greens tossed in sherry or balsamic vinegar with additional sliced fresh mushrooms.

4 eggs
2 tbs. dry sherry
1 tsp. freshly grated nutmeg
salt and white pepper to taste
3 tbs. unsalted butter
1/4 cup chopped shallots
1 cup thinly sliced white mushrooms
1 cup thinly sliced wild mushrooms, such as shiitake or cremini
2 tbs. chopped fresh flat-leaf parsley
one 9-inch frozen pie shell, thawed
1 cup shredded Gruyère or Swiss cheese
1/2 cup grated Parmesan cheese

Heat oven to 450°. In a medium bowl, lightly beat eggs, sherry, nutmeg, salt and pepper; set aside. In a skillet over medium heat, melt butter and sauté shallots, mushrooms and parsley for 5 to 7 minutes, until mushrooms are tender and liquid has evaporated. Place in bottom of pie shell and sprinkle with cheeses. Carefully pour egg mixture over mushroom-cheese mixture. Lower oven temperature to 425° and bake quiche for 35 to 40 minutes, or until golden brown.

QUICHE GUADALAJARA

Servings: 12

An easy-to-prepare Mexican pie stands out as a festive centerpiece. Prepare a salad filled with tomatoes, black olives and fresh corn kernels as a side dish. Chorizo is a spicy Mexican sausage that can be found at a reliable butcher.

3/4 lb. chorizo, casings removed
1/2 lb. ground beef
1 1/2 cups chopped onions
1 pkg. (1.5 oz.) taco seasoning mix
1 can (16 oz.) reduced-fat refried beans
1 can (4 oz.) diced green chiles, drained
1 cup sliced California black olives
two 9-inch frozen pie shells, thawed
2 cups shredded reduced-fat Monterey Jack cheese
2 cups shredded reduced-fat cheddar cheese
8 eggs, beaten
nonfat sour cream
prepared guacamole
blue corn chips

Heat oven to 350°. In a skillet over medium-high heat, cook chorizo, beef and onions for about 10 minutes, or until meats are no longer pink. Remove from heat. Drain fat and add taco seasoning. Mix well and set aside. Layer 1/2 of the beans, cheeses, chiles, olives and meat mixture on each pie crust. Pour 1/2 of the egg mixture over each pie crust. Bake for 30 minutes until set and golden brown; cool. Serve with sour cream, guacamole and blue corn chips on the side.

WINE AND CHEESE TORTA

Servings: 12

This Italian-style savory pie is just right for sophisticated parties and feeds a crowd. A hearty green leaf salad completes this carefree entrée.

6 tbs. unsalted butter, melted
1 loaf day-old French bread, cut into cubes
½ lb. Monterey Jack cheese, shredded
1 lb. Swiss cheese, shredded
¼ lb. Italian salami, coarsely chopped
12 eggs
3½ cups milk
1 cup dry white wine
4 green onions, minced
2 tbs. chopped fresh tarragon leaves
1 tbs. Dijon-style mustard
salt and pepper to taste
1½ cups nonfat sour cream
1 cup grated Parmesan cheese

Butter two 9-x13-inch baking dishes. Spread bread cubes in bottom of each dish and drizzle with melted butter. Sprinkle with cheeses. In a large bowl, beat eggs, milk, wine, onions, tarragon, mustard, salt and pepper. Pour over cheese and salami layer. Cover tightly with foil and and refrigerate for 24 hours.

Heat oven to 350° and remove torta from refrigerator. Bake covered for 1 hour , until bubbly. Remove from oven. Uncover; spread with sour cream and Parmesan cheese. Return to oven and bake for about 10 minutes uncovered, until crusty and light brown in color.

JAPANESE NIMONO

Servings: 6

Communal cooking pots (nimono) are popular in Japan. Vegetables, meats, seafood and tofu are cooked tableside, dipped into sauces and served with rice. It is believed that old friendships strengthen and new ones bloom when people dine in this fashion.

1 lb. napa cabbage, cored and thinly sliced
1 lb. asparagus, cut into 1/4-inch diagonal pieces
2 medium carrots, peeled and cut into 1/4-inch diagonal pieces
1 bunch green onions, cut into 1/4-inch diagonal pieces
1/4 lb. snow peas
8 medium shiitake mushrooms, sliced
1 lb. medium raw shrimp, shelled
1 lb. bay scallops
1 pkg. (14-16 oz.) regular Japanese style tofu
4 slices fresh ginger
6 cups chicken broth
plum sauce, soy sauce and hoisin sauce
hot steamed jasmine rice

On a platter, arrange vegetables, seafood and tofu. In an electric skillet or wok set at medium-high heat, cook ginger slices in chicken broth for 3 to 5 minutes, or until fragrant. Remove ginger and discard. Lower heat to medium. Cook vegetables and seafood in hot broth. Allow each guest to remove food as it cooks, dip into sauces and eat with rice. When all ingredients are used, ladle broth into rice bowls and drink.

VEGETABLES WITH ANCHOVIES AND GARLIC

Servings: 4

"Bagna cauda," or "warm bath" is a northern Italian specialty dish that is fun to eat. Family and friends gather around the table and dip an assortment of tender, young vegetables in a bubbling garlicky-anchovy bath.

¼ cup extra virgin olive oil
½ cup butter
4 cloves garlic, finely chopped
1 can (2 oz.) anchovy fillets
¼ cup minced fresh flat-leaf parsley
2 red bell peppers, stemmed, seeded and cut into 1½-inch slices
2 green bell peppers, stemmed, seeded and cut into 1½-inch slices
1 lb. whole white mushrooms
1 small head cauliflower, cut into florets
1 small head broccoli, cut into florets
3 small zucchini, cut into ½-inch pieces
½ lb. green beans, cut into 1-inch pieces
½ lb. cherry tomatoes
one large loaf Italian bread, sliced

In a heavy skillet, heat olive oil and butter. Sauté garlic, taking care not to brown. Add anchovies, breaking up fillets with a wooden spoon and cooking gently until dissolved. Immediately pour sauce into a chafing dish and keep hot. Arrange vegetables on a platter with fondue forks or long cocktail bamboo skewers. Spear vegetables, swirl in hot anchovy sauce and eat with bread.

ROAST STUFFED PUMPKIN

Servings: 6

Ideal for a vegetarian entrée, this savory filling is rich with fruit, nuts, herbs and spices, complementing the mellow taste of slow-roasted pumpkin.

1 pumpkin, 10 inches in diameter
½ cup butter, plus more for scattering
2 cups coarsely chopped onions
4 cloves garlic, minced
1 cup coarsely chopped celery with leaves
1 cup thinly sliced mushrooms
¼ cup chopped fresh flat-leaf parsley
2 tbs. poultry seasoning
1 tsp. dried oregano
1 tsp dried sage
1 tsp. ground cumin
½ tsp. ground ginger
½ tsp. cinnamon
½ tsp. nutmeg
½ tsp. ground cloves
salt and pepper to taste
2 large eggs, beaten
1 cup vegetable broth
1 cup dry sherry
6-8 cups dry wheat bread, cut into cubes
½ cup chopped walnuts
½ cup chopped almonds
½ cup chopped hazelnuts
½ cup chopped Brazil nuts
1 cup peeled, chopped apples
½ cup raisins

Prepare pumpkin by cutting a large circle around stem. Lift and discard top. Remove seeds and fibers. Set prepared pumpkin aside.

In a large microwave-safe bowl, melt butter. Add onions, garlic, celery, mushrooms and parsley with poultry seasoning, oregano, sage, cumin, ginger, cinnamon, nutmeg, cloves, salt and pepper; mix well. Cover and microwave on HIGH for 8 to 10 minutes, until vegetables are tender. Carefully remove cover and cool.

When cool, stir in beaten eggs, broth and sherry. Add bread cubes, nuts and fruit, stirring until bread softens and moisture is absorbed. Stuffing should be moist.

Heat oven to 350°. Fill pumpkin with stuffing, taking care not to pack tightly since stuffing will expand as it cooks. With a sharp knife, make several slits at different levels in wall of pumpkin. Cut slivers from extra butter and push into slits. Scatter butter slivers over top of stuffing. Cover exposed stuffing with foil. Place filled pumpkin in a greased baking pan and bake for 1 hour.

Remove foil and resume baking for about 1½ hours until skin is dark orange and exposed stuffing is brown and crisp. Remove from oven and cool for 20 minutes before serving.

VEGETABLE CURRY

Servings: 6

This curry can be made with assorted root, vine or bush vegetables. The broth has some heat, but it's not overpowering. The coconut milk tames the spiciness of the curry and cayenne.

1 cup peeled, thinly sliced carrots
1 cup peeled, thinly sliced potatoes
1 cup broccoli florets
1 cup cauliflower florets
1/2 cup green beans
1/2 cup thinly sliced red bell pepper
2 cups thinly sliced zucchini
2 cups thinly sliced mushrooms
1/4 cup canola oil
1 tsp. mustard seeds
1 tsp. cumin seeds
2 tbs. minced fresh ginger
1 large onion, thinly sliced
2 large cloves garlic, minced
3/4 tsp. cayenne pepper
2 tsp. salt
3 tsp. curry powder
1 tsp. ground cardamom
1 tsp. cinnamon
1 tbs. brown sugar
1 can (10.5 oz.) diced tomatoes
1 can (14 oz.) coconut milk
2 tbs. prepared mango chutney
2/3 cup chopped fresh basil leaves
6 cups steamed basmati rice
2 limes, cut into wedges
salted peanuts, shredded coconut and raisins for garnish

Microwave vegetables on HIGH in batches until tender-crisp. Time will vary according to power of oven. Do not fully cook. Set aside.

In a large, deep skillet, heat 2 tbs. of the oil. Over low heat, stir mustard and cumin seeds until fragrant. Add remaining 2 tbs. oil to skillet and stir-fry ginger, onion, garlic, pepper, salt, curry powder, cardamom and cinnamon until spices blend and onions wilt. Fold in vegetables, brown sugar, tomatoes and coconut milk. Bring to a boil, lower heat to simmer, cover and cook for about 15 to 20 minutes, just until vegetables are tender and heated through. Stir in chutney and basil. Serve over rice garnished with lime wedges. Pass salted peanuts, raisins and coconut for sprinkling.

LINGUINI WITH MONKFISH AND OLIVES

Servings: 6

Monkfish, also known as angler fish, is a firm-textured, low-fat substitute for lobster. It lends itself well to this Italian stir-fry with olives, capers, garden tomatoes and basil. Dress an arugula salad with a few olives, oranges, lemon and sliced red onion. A selection of Italian cheese and fresh fruit help to send this meal into overtime.

1 lb. fresh linguini
1/4 cup extra virgin olive oil
4 cloves garlic, mashed
4 sprigs fresh thyme
1 1/2 lb. monkfish, cut into cubes
1 cup pitted kalamata olives
2 tbs. salted capers, rinsed and drained
2 cups chopped mixed red and yellow pear-shaped tomatoes
2 cups coarsely torn fresh basil leaves
salt and pepper to taste

In a large pot of salted water, cook linguini for 4 minutes, until tender but firm to the bite, *al dente*. Drain, reserving 1 cup of the cooking water, and keep warm.

Heat oil in large skillet over medium-high heat. Add garlic and thyme and sauté. Discard garlic and turn heat to high. Add monkfish and stir-fry for 4 minutes. Add olives, capers, tomatoes, 1 cup of the basil, cooked linguini and reserved cooking water. Cook over high heat for about 1 minute, stirring constantly, until thick sauce forms. Add remaining 1 cup basil and season with salt and pepper. Serve immediately.

SMOKED SALMON LASAGNE

Servings: 6-8

A cheesy white sauce is the base for this unusual seafood lasagna. The contrast of flavor, texture and color make this simple dish company fare. Serve with a salad featuring all green vegetables – asparagus tips, zucchini slices, snap beans and broccoli.

½ cup unsalted butter
⅓ cup flour
1 qt. milk
1 tsp. salt
½ tsp. white pepper
¼ cup grated Parmesan cheese
¼ cup grated Gruyère cheese
¼ cup dry sherry
1 cup shredded mozzarella cheese
1 cup shredded provolone cheese
1½ cups grated Romano cheese
1 lb. spinach lasagna noodles
3 cups chopped, peeled, seeded tomatoes, drained
3 cups thinly sliced mushrooms
1 lb. smoked salmon, chopped

In a medium saucepan, melt butter over low heat. Add flour and cook for 3 minutes, stirring constantly. Whisk in milk and bring to a boil. Cook for 8 to 10 minutes over medium-high heat, whisking constantly, until thick. Remove from heat and stir in salt, pepper, Parmesan, Gruyère and sherry. In a large bowl, combine mozzarella, provolone and Romano; set aside.

Heat oven to 350°. Lightly oil a 13-x-9-x-2-inch pan. Layer prepared pan with 1/3 of the noodles, cheese mixture, tomatoes and mushrooms. Pour 1/3 of the sauce mixture over. Repeat layering, ending with remaining cheese mixture. Bake for about 45 to 60 minutes, or until top is golden brown. Let stand for 15 minutes before serving.

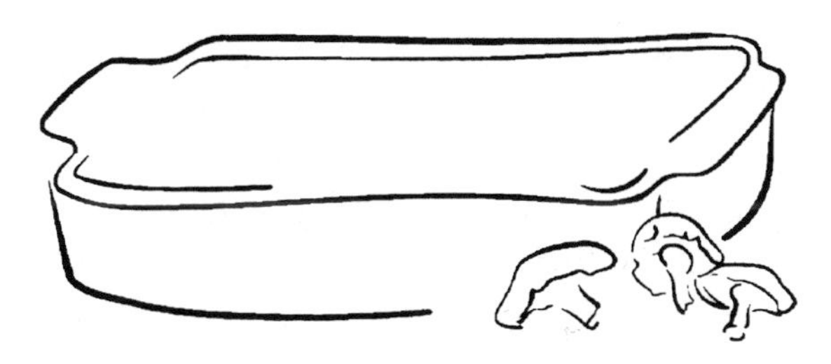

IMPROMPTU SHRIMP ALFREDO

Servings: 6-8

This meal takes less than 30 minutes from freezer to table. The secret is having some essential staples in the house.

2 lb. frozen, peeled, cooked baby shrimp
1 cup dry white wine
1 shallot, quartered
3 tbs. instant flour
2 cups half-and-half
2 cups frozen peas
2 tbs. unsalted butter
1½ cups grated Parmesan cheese, plus more for sprinkling
2 tsp. grated fresh lemon peel (zest)
1 tbs. chopped fresh basil leaves
salt and white pepper to taste
hot cooked fettuccine, cooking water reserved

In a large skillet over high heat, add frozen shrimp, white wine and shallots. Cover and bring to a boil. Lower heat to medium-high and cook for 4 minutes, or until shrimp are heated through. Discard shallot and set aside shrimp. Shake flour directly into pan, whisking constantly so lumps do not form and mixture thickens. Gradually whisk in half-and-half to dilute sauce. Add frozen peas and cook until peas are warm. Stir in shrimp, butter, cheese, lemon zest, basil, salt and pepper and continue to cook. Sauce should be thick and smooth. Fold in fettuccine, adding reserved pasta water if sauce is too thick. Serve and sprinkle with extra cheese.

RIGATONI BAKE

Servings: 12-16

Prepared foods are the tricks of the cooking trade here. This recipe makes two 9-x-14-x-2-inch pans, enough to serve a large group with ease.

3/4 lb. Italian-style sausage
2 jars (26 oz. each) Bolognese sauce
2 cups water
2 tbs. dried oregano
2 tsp. fennel seeds
1 cup fresh basil leaves
1 lb. dried rigatoni
1 pkg. (1½ lb.) frozen cooked Italian-style meatballs, chopped
2 cans (4 oz. each) sliced mushrooms, drained
1 lb. mozzarella cheese, cut into cubes
1 pkg. (2 lb.) ricotta cheese
1 cup grated Parmesan cheese

Heat broiler to 500°. Broil sausage 4 inches from heating element until brown, about 8 minutes. Drain, chop coarsely and set aside. Heat oven to 350°. In a large bowl, mix sauce, water, oregano, fennel and basil leaves. In 2 oiled, nonmetal 9-x-13 pans, ladle tomato mixture, covering bottom of pans. Layer dry rigatoni, meat mixture, sausage, mushrooms, mozzarella and spoonfuls of ricotta. Do not crowd rigatoni when layering. Pour tomato mixture over each completed layer. Sprinkle with Romano cheese. Cover with foil and bake until bubbling, about 50 minutes. Remove foil and bake until surface browns, about 20 minutes. Allow to rest for 15 minutes for easier cutting.

MUSSELS AND SHRIMP PILAF

Servings: 4

Quick-cooking brown rice and thin spaghetti form a colorful, company seafood pilaf. Similar spice accents of ginger and cilantro can be used in an accompanying green salad. Look for shrimp bouillon cubes in the Asian section of the supermarket.

1½ lb. mussels
1 lb. medium shrimp
1 large shallot, chopped
2 tbs. chopped fresh ginger
1 cup fresh cilantro leaves and stems, plus more for garnish
½ tsp. red pepper flakes
1½ cups dry white wine
¼ cup water
1 shrimp bouillon cube
2 tsp. peanut oil
3 oz. thin spaghetti, broken into 1-inch pieces (about 1 cup)
2 cups instant brown rice
2 cups frozen peas, thawed

Clean mussels by scrubbing and removing beards. Place mussels in bowl filled with cold water. Clean unshelled shrimp by rinsing under running water. Add to mussels.

In a large skillet over medium-high heat, combine shallot, ginger, cilantro, red pepper flakes and wine. Drain mussels and shrimp and add to skillet. Cover and bring to a boil. Cook for about 3 to 5 minutes, until mussels open and shrimp are pink. Remove to a bowl and keep warm. Strain broth into a measuring cup. Add water to make 2½ cups. Dissolve shrimp bouillon cube in broth mixture. Wipe out skillet. Heat oil and stir-fry spaghetti and rice for 3 to 5 minutes, until golden brown. Pour broth mixture over rice; lower heat to simmer and cook for 8 minutes, or until rice is nearly cooked. Shell all of the shrimp and all but 16 of the mussels. Add seafood and thawed peas to skillet. Cover and heat through. Serve garnished with additional cilantro.

FRUITED PHEASANT

Servings: 4-6

A rich glaze of plum jam, soy, Worcestershire, and honey sweetens the gamy taste of this bird. Prunes and pistachios flavor the couscous.

1 young pheasant, about 3½lb. rinsed and dried
1 carrot, peeled and cut into ¼-inch slices
1 onion, cut into ¼-inch slices
4 cloves garlic, cut into slivers
4 sprigs fresh tarragon
3 tbs. plum jam
1 tbs. soy sauce
1 tbs. Worcestershire sauce
1 tsp. honey
½ cup white wine
1½ cups instant couscous
1¼ cups boiling water
2 tbs. unsalted butter
10 prunes, cut into slivers
¼ cup shelled pistachio nuts
1½ cups finely chopped green onions

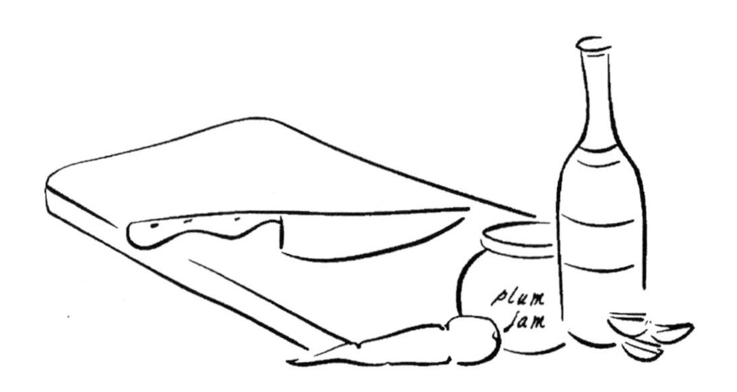

Heat oven to 350°. Lightly sprinkle cavity with salt and stuff with 3/4 of the carrot, onion, garlic and tarragon. Combine jam, soy, Worcestershire sauce and honey, and brush pheasant with mixture. In a shallow baking pan, place pheasant on a bed of remaining 1/4 of the vegetable and herb mixture. Pour wine over, and roast uncovered for 1 3/4 hours, or until internal temperature taken in the meatiest part of the thigh reaches 180°. Remove bird from oven; place on carving board. Let rest for about 10 minutes before carving meat from bones. Set meat aside.

In a saucepan over medium-high heat, cook down juices until syrupy. Strain into a bowl and keep warm. Place couscous into a shallow bowl. Stir in boiling water and butter. Cover and let stand until couscous has absorbed all water. Separate grains with a fork and stir in plums and pistachio nuts. Arrange on a heated platter. Mound pheasant slices in center, arranging crisp-skinned pieces on top. Spoon syrupy drippings over pheasant and top with green onions.

CHICKEN AND TOMATILLO TACOS

Servings: 10-12

Corn tortillas are used to sandwich this spicy chicken filling. Accompany the tacos with bowls of grated cheese, salsa, sliced green onions, diced avocado, fresh cilantro leaves and lime wedges for a fiesta. Use the meat from 4 whole, poached chicken breasts.

1/2 cup coarsely chopped almonds
1/2 cup coarsely chopped pecans
2 cups hulled green pumpkin seeds
1 can (28 oz.) tomatillos, drained
5 serrano chiles, seeded
1 large onion, thinly sliced
4 cloves garlic
1 cup cilantro leaves, tightly packed plus more for garnish
1/4 cup vegetable oil
2 cups chicken broth
1 tsp. ground cumin
1/2 tsp. cinnamon
1/2 tsp. ground cloves
2 tsp. ground allspice
1 poblano chile, roasted, peeled and diced
1 1/2 lb. cooked chicken, shredded
2 cans (15.25 oz. each) reduced-sodium kidney beans, rinsed and drained
juice of 2 limes
corn tortillas

In a large skillet over medium heat, toast almonds, pecans and pumpkin seeds for about 5 minutes, stirring constantly, until brown; remove and cool. In an electric spice grinder, in several batches, grind 1½ cups nut mixture to a powder. In a food processor workbowl, place tomatillos, serrano chiles, onion, garlic and ½ cup of the cilantro. Process until blended, but still chunky. In same skillet, simmer tomatillo mixture in oil for 10 minutes, stirring occasionally. Add 1½ cups of the broth, powdered nut and seed mixture, cumin, cinnamon, cloves and allspice. Simmer sauce for about 15 minutes, stirring frequently, until slightly thickened. Stir in remaining ½ cup cilantro and broth, poblano chile, chicken and kidney beans. Simmer until heated through. Fold in remaining 1½ cups nut mixture and lime juice. Garnish with additional cilantro and serve with warm corn tortillas.

TANDOORI CHICKEN

Servings: 8

Cooking in a tandoori oven, a pit-ike clay oven, is the traditional method of roasting in India. Food is placed directly on the oven surface and heated to extreme temperatures. Tandoori paste (available at gourmet food markets and Indian markets) is rubbed into the surface of the meats or poultry or mixed with yogurt for a marinade. The tandoori item is usually served with naan, a flatbread baked in the same oven. You can also find it at gourmet shops or an Indian grocery.

1 cup nonfat plain yogurt
1 jar (11 oz.) tandoori paste
8 chicken breasts, skinned and boned
1/2 cup vegetable oil
2 large onions, chopped
3 large tomatoes, chopped
3 large green bell peppers, stemmed, seeded and chopped
8 cups hot cooked basmati rice
cilantro sprigs for garnish
peanuts, chutney, grated coconut and plain yogurt for accompaniments
naan bread, optional

Place chicken breasts in a large bowl. Mix yogurt and tandoori paste and coat chicken breasts with the mixture. Cover bowl and refrigerate overnight.

Heat oven to 350°. Remove chicken from marinade and let drain on a rack. Coat bottom of an open roasting pan with 1/4 cup of the oil. Layer pan with onion, tomatoes and peppers. Place drained chicken over vegetables. Drizzle with remaining 1/4 cup oil. Bake for 20 to 30 minutes, until chicken is no longer pink and vegetables are cooked. Serve with rice, garnish with cilantro and pass peanuts, chutney, coconut and yogurt.

AEGEAN LAMB STEW

Servings: 6

Ground lamb, vegetables, tiny pasta and fragrant spices simmer together to produce a robust, healthful dinner. Serve with a cool cucumber and yogurt salad flavored with garlic and mint for a taste from the Greek Isles.

1½ lb. ground lamb
4 tsp. garlic powder
salt and pepper to taste
6 cups sliced mixed vegetables, such as eggplant, zucchini or yellow squash, ½-inch-thick slices
1 red onion, cut into ½-inch-thick slices
1 cup mixed red, green and yellow bell pepper slices
1 tbs. fresh thyme leaves
¼ cup fresh oregano leaves
¼ cup extra virgin olive oil
3 cloves garlic, minced
1 can (14.5 oz.) cut tomatoes with juice
1 tsp. ground allspice
1 tsp. cinnamon
3 whole cloves
1 cup pitted kalamata olives
1 cup orzo (teardrop-shaped pasta)
1 can (14.5 oz.) beef broth, defatted
½ cup water
1 cup crumbled feta cheese
1 cup chopped fresh flat-leaf parsley

Heat broiler. Season lamb with garlic powder, salt and pepper. Shape into two 1½-inch-thick logs and place on a foil lined baking sheet. Broil for 6 minutes, turning midway through the cooking process. Remove from baking sheet; drain and discard fat drippings. With a fork, break logs into large chunks and set aside. Place new sheet of foil on baking sheet. Arrange vegetable and onion slices with herbs on sheet. Drizzle with 2 tbs. of the olive oil. Broil about 6 minutes, until vegetables are tender, turning once; set aside.

Heat oven to 400°. In large Dutch oven, sauté garlic in remaining 2 tbs. olive oil. Stir in tomatoes with juice and spices. Cook over medium heat for 3 to 5 minutes. Add lamb, vegetables, olives and orzo. Pour in beef broth and water and stir well. Cover and bring to a simmer. Remove from stove and place in oven. Bake until most of the liquid is absorbed, about 30 to 35 minutes. Remove cloves and top with cheese and parsley.

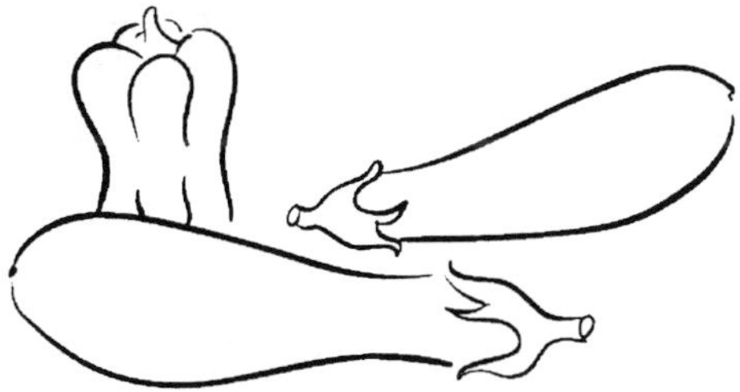

FAMILY FAVORITES

VEGETABLE BEAN SOUP

Servings: 10-12

This soup is a time-saver, and will leave you with extra for weeknight meals. Break off pieces from a baguette and soak up the tomato juices left in the bowl.

10 cups cold water
½ lb. small dried white beans
⅓ cup olive oil
1 medium onion, chopped
2 stalks celery, chopped
2 large carrots, peeled and chopped
1 tbs. dried rosemary
1 tbs. dried sage
1 tbs. dried parsley
1 bay leaf
3 whole allspice berries
4 vegetarian bouillon cubes
1 can (10.75 oz.) tomato soup
salt and pepper to taste
1 can (15.5 oz.) garbanzo beans, drained
1 can (15.5 oz.) kidney beans, drained
1 can (15.5 oz.) black beans, drained
2 cooked cups elbow macaroni

Fill a pot with cold water, add beans and boil for 2 minutes. Remove from heat, let stand 1 hour and drain; set aside. In a pot over medium heat, sauté vegetables in olive oil for 5 to 7 minutes until soft. Add drained beans to pot with fresh water, herbs, bay leaf, allspice, bouillon cubes, tomato soup, salt and pepper. Bring to a boil and skim foam from surface. Remove bay leaf, lower heat and simmer for 1½ hours, or until beans are tender. Add beans and macaroni and heat through.

PORK AND BEAN SOUP

Servings: 6-8

Save the bones when cooking pork loin roast. They can be part of the base for an interesting soup. Vary the seasonings and the beans for different ethnic flavors. Here, cumin, allspice, nutmeg and cloves bring the flavor of the Eastern Mediterranean into your kitchen.

6 qt. cold water
bones from pork loin roast
3 large stalks celery, cut into 1½ inch pieces
4 large carrots, peeled and cut into 1½-inch pieces
3 Yukon Gold potatoes, quartered
4 cloves garlic, sliced
1 large onion, quartered
1 bay leaf
1 tsp. ground cumin
1 tsp. ground allspice
1 tbs. hot Spanish or Hungarian paprika
¼ tsp. red pepper flakes
1 tsp. ground cloves
1 tsp. ground nutmeg
2 tsp. salt
1 beef bouillon cube
1 vegetable bouillon cube
1 cup bite-sized pieces cooked pork roast, or more to taste
1 can (14 oz.) garbanzo beans, rinsed and drained
1 can (14 oz.) fava beans, rinsed and drained
1 can (14 oz.) kidney beans, rinsed and drained
2 cups slivered Swiss chard leaves

In a large stockpot, bring water and pork bones to a boil. Simmer for 30 minutes, skimming surface to remove scum. Add celery, carrots, potatoes, garlic, onion, bay leaf, cumin, allspice, paprika, red pepper flakes, cloves, nutmeg, and salt to pot. Cover pot and simmer for 1½ hours, until thickened. Add beef and vegetable bouillon cubes. Also add leftover pork, garbanzo, fava and kidney beans. Simmer for an additional 30 minutes. Before serving, remove bones and whole spices and add Swiss chard leaves. Cook until leaves wilt and turn bright green. Ladle into soup bowls and serve.

SIZZLING TORTILLA SOUP

Servings: 4

Heating the tortilla chips before crumbling into this hearty Mexican vegetable soup creates a sizzle sound. The avocado and cheese slices lining the soup bowl are a nice surprise. The array of condiments served with the soup makes it a treat.

2 tbs. extra virgin olive oil
2 cloves garlic, chopped
1 large onion, thinly sliced
1 tbs. dried oregano
1 tbs. dried thyme
6 cups vegetable broth
1 can (16 oz.) chopped tomatoes
3 carrots, peeled and thinly sliced
2 white potatoes, peeled and diced
1 sweet potato, peeled, diced
1 cup fresh or canned corn kernels,
1 green bell pepper, cut into thin strips
1 tsp. salt
1 tsp. sugar
3/4 tsp. pepper
2 large ripe avocados, sliced
2 cups shredded reduced-fat Monterey Jack cheese
2 cups shredded cheddar cheese
6 cups tortilla chips
lime slices for garnish
2 cups fresh cilantro leaves

In a large stockpot over medium heat, heat oil. Sauté garlic, onion, oregano and thyme for 10 minutes, until onion is soft and herbs are fragrant. Add broth, tomatoes with juice, carrots, white and sweet potatoes, corn, green pepper, salt, sugar and pepper. Bring to a boil. Cover, lower heat and simmer for 30 minutes, or until vegetables are cooked through. Prepare 4 soup bowls by lining bottoms with avocado slices and cheeses. Ladle soup into bowls and top with cilantro. "Sizzle soup" by adding hot, crushed tortilla chips and garnish with lime wedges.

ZUCCHINI QUICHE

Serves: 6-8

This is an updated version of a 1960's dish that was popular when vegetarian entrées were first featured in Northern California restaurants. If you don't want to make homemade crust, use two prepared 9-inch pie crusts, thawed, if frozen.

2 cups all-purpose flour
½ tsp. salt
½ tsp. sugar
¾ cup cold unsalted butter,
  cut into pieces
lemon juice
1-3 tbs. ice water

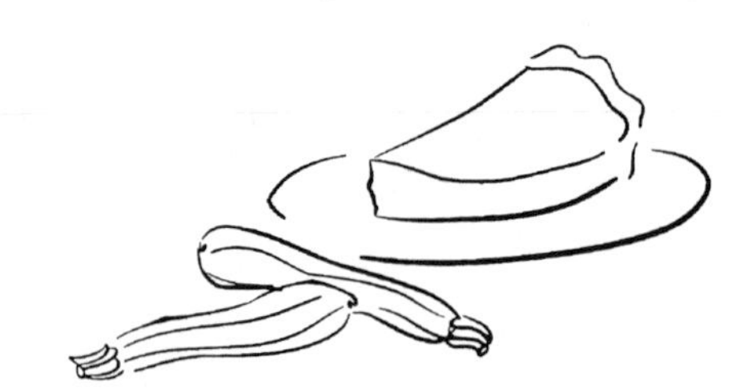

For dough, mix flour, salt and sugar together in a large bowl. Cut butter with a pastry cutter or two knives into a cornmeal-like consistency. Sprinkle with a few drops of lemon juice and water, repeating until dough clings together in a ball. Divide in half. Place each half between two layers of wax paper and press into a disc; chill until ready to use.

ZUCCHINI FILLING

Servings: 4

2 eggs, separated
1½ cups low-fat sour cream
2 tbs. chopped fresh basil
2 tbs. chopped fresh chives
2 tbs. flour
salt and white pepper to taste
2 lb. small zucchini, cut into ¼-inch-thick slices
¼ cup shredded cheddar cheese
¼ cup grated Parmesan cheese
1½ cups fresh breadcrumbs
¼ cup cold butter

Heat oven to 450°. In a large bowl, beat egg yolks with sour cream until well blended. Fold in basil, chives, flour, salt and pepper; set aside. In a small bowl, beat egg whites until stiff. Fold into sour cream mixture; set aside. If making crusts, roll out between layers of wax paper. Line two 9-inch pie tins. Layer zucchini slices and sour cream mixture in each pie shell, ending with sour cream mixture. Sprinkle combined cheeses and breadcrumbs over each. Top with slivers of butter. Bake for 10 minutes. Reduce oven temperature to 325°. Bake for about 40 minutes until golden brown.

ARTICHOKE CHICKEN

Servings: 6-8

The combination of artichokes and chicken is magical. This presentation is simple, but elegant. Serve with whole cranberry sauce and crusty rolls.

1 fryer chicken, about 3½ lb.
flour seasoned with salt and pepper
¼ cup extra virgin olive oil
1 pkg. (8 oz.) frozen artichoke hearts, cut into quarters
3 shallots, minced
2 cups sliced mushrooms
1 cup dry white wine
2 cups chicken broth
3 tbs. chopped fresh tarragon leaves
4 sprigs tarragon for garnish
6 cups prepared rice pilaf

Prepare chicken by cutting breasts in half cross-wise, disjointing thighs from legs and saving backs and wings for stock. Season with flour mixture. In a large skillet, heat 2 tbs. of the oil to medium-high and brown floured chicken parts. Push to side, add remaining 2 tbs. oil and add frozen artichoke hearts, cooking briefly. Add shallots, mushrooms, wine, chicken broth and tarragon leaves. Bring to a boil. Reduce heat, cover and simmer for 40 minutes, or until chicken is tender. Serve over rice garnished with tarragon sprigs.

BAKED PENNE WITH HAM, CHEESE AND PEAS

Servings: 4

This is an easy Sunday supper that is nourishing as well as good-tasting. A seasonal salad, dinner rolls and chocolate brownies complete this meal.

2 cans (12 oz.) nonfat evaporated milk
2½ cups water
2 eggs
1 tsp. ground sage
salt and pepper to taste
½ lb. dried penne pasta
1 cup shredded sharp cheddar cheese
1 cup shredded Monterey Jack cheese
1 cup cubed smoked ham
2 cups frozen peas
¼ cup chopped flat-leaf fresh parsley

In a food processor workbowl or blender container, process milk, water, eggs, sage, salt and pepper until well processed; set aside. In an oiled 9-x-13-inch pan, build layers of pasta, cheeses, ham, peas and parsley, ending with layer of cheese. Pour milk-egg mixture over, making sure liquid reaches bottom of pan and some pasta is above liquid level.

Heat oven to 350°. Wrap in foil and bake until bubbly, about 40 minutes. Remove foil and continue baking until pasta top is crisp and cheese is melted. Remove from oven and let stand for 10 minutes before serving.

BAKED SALMON WITH VEGETABLES

Servings: 4

The mild taste of the salmon is complemented by the savory vegetables as they bake together under a Parmesan breadcrumb topping. A crisp radish and cucumber salad and a warmed bakery fruit pie complete this meal.

2 cups fresh or canned corn kernels
2 cups diced, peeled baking potatoes
1½ cups sliced green beans
½ cup diced green bell pepper
½ cup chopped fresh sage leaves, or 2 tsp. dried
½ cup chopped fresh flat-leaf parsley
salt and pepper to taste
¼ cup extra virgin olive oil
3 tbs. minced onion
4 salmon steaks or fillets, about 4 oz. each
2-3 large tomatoes, thinly sliced
1 cup breadcrumbs mixed with ¼ cup olive oil
1 tbs. minced garlic
2 tbs. grated Parmesan cheese

Heat oven to 350°. In a well-greased 1½-quart casserole, arrange corn, potatoes and beans, sprinkling each layer with green pepper, sage, ¼ cup of the parsley, salt and pepper. Combine oil with onion. Dip salmon pieces in mixture and place on top of vegetables. Arrange tomato slices over salmon. Mix remaining ½ cup parsley with breadcrumbs, olive oil, garlic and cheese and sprinkle over tomato slices. Drizzle remaining oil-onion mixture over crumbs. Bake for 1 hour, until vegetables are tender and fish falls apart easily when cut with a fork.

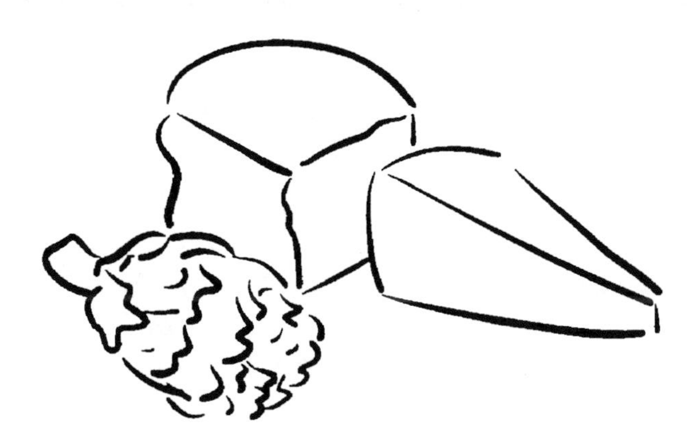

CHINESE CHICKEN CASSEROLE

Servings: 4

Leftover chicken pleases even the most disciminating tastes with this mild and exotic dish.

3 cups cooked chicken cubes
2 tsp. lemon juice
1 tbs. soy sauce
1/4 cup chopped green onions
1 cup chopped celery
1 medium red bell pepper, stemmed, seeded and cut into 1/4-inch dice
1 cup slivered snow peas
1 cup whole button mushrooms
1/2 lb. bean sprouts
1 can (5 oz.) sliced water chestnuts, drained and diced
1 cup low-fat mayonnaise
1 can (3 oz.) chow mein noodles
1/4 cup toasted slivered almonds

Sprinkle chicken with lemon juice and soy sauce. Cover and refrigerate overnight.

Heat oven to 350°. Combine chicken with onions, celery, pepper, snow peas, mushrooms, bean sprouts, water chestnuts and mayonnaise. Mix well and turn chicken mixture into a nonstick sprayed 1½-quart casserole. Sprinkle noodles on top and bake for 25 minutes, or until heated through and noodles are crispy. Remove from oven, sprinkle with toasted almonds and serve.

TORTILLA CHICKEN CASSEROLE

Servings: 4

A bag of boneless chicken breasts in the freezer and several varieties of canned soups in the pantry ensure a hassle-free dinner on those days when everything seems to go wrong.

1 jar (16 oz.) salsa
1 can (10.75 oz.) reduced-fat cream of chicken soup
1 can (10.75 oz.) reduced-fat cream of celery or cream of mushroom soup
1 cup nonfat milk
5 boneless chicken breast halves, cooked and coarsely chopped
1 lb. reduced-fat cheddar cheese, shredded
12 corn tortillas, cut into bite-sized pieces

Heat oven to 300°. In a large bowl, whisk salsa, soups and milk to form sauce. In a greased 2-quart casserole, layer with 1/3 of the sauce, tortillas, chicken and cheese. Repeat layering, ending with cheese. Bake uncovered for 1½ hours, or until heated through and top layer of cheese is bubbly and golden. Let stand for 8 to 10 minutes to thicken.

TUNA CASSEROLE

Servings: 4

There must be as many versions of this popular dish as there are cooks who prepare it. Tuna casserole is economical, easy to prepare and is delicious. If you do not have your own recipe, this one may earn family-favorite status.

2 cans (10 oz. each) low fat cream of mushroom soup
4½ cups cold water
½ cup dry sherry
4 cups cooked wide egg noodles
2 cans (6 oz. each) water-packed white tuna
2 cups frozen peas
1½ cups thinly sliced mushrooms
1 cup shredded Monterey Jack cheese
2 cups shredded extra-sharp cheddar cheese
4 cups crushed potato chips
¼ cup chopped fresh flat-leaf parsley
paprika for sprinkling

Heat oven to 350°. In a large bowl, whisk soup, water and sherry; set aside. In an oiled 7-x-10 or 1½-quart baking pan, layer ½ of the noodles, tuna, peas, mushrooms and cheeses, ending with a layer of cheese. Pour ½ of the soup mixture over the other ingredients, making sure liquid completely covers dry ingredients. Repeat with remaining noodles, tuna, peas and mushrooms. Pour remaining ½ of soup mixture over dry ingredients. Sprinkle with remaining cheeses. Mix chips with parsley and pat over surface of casserole. Sprinkle with paprika. Cover with foil and bake until casserole bubbles, about 20 minutes. Remove foil and bake for 8 to 10 minutes until chips are crisp and brown.

BACON-WRAPPED MEAT LOAF WITH ROASTED VEGETABLES

Servings: 6

Every cook prepares meat loaf a little differently. This version is a basic one, but instead of baking in a loaf pan, ours is shaped into an oval and baked on a rimmed baking sheet surrounded by vegetables.

1 lb. ground veal
1 lb. ground pork
1 lb. ground beef
½ cup fresh breadcrumbs, soaked in beef broth and squeezed dry
1 medium onion, finely minced
¾ cup chopped fresh flat-leaf parsley
2 tsp. chopped fresh rosemary
2 tsp. chopped fresh marjoram
2 tsp. chopped fresh thyme
salt and pepper to taste
2 eggs, beaten
5 slices bacon
1 pkg. (10 oz.) frozen petite whole onions
1 pkg. (16 oz.) frozen baby carrots
12 tiny creamer potatoes, par-boiled

Heat oven to 325°. In a large bowl, mix meats, breadcrumbs, onion, ½ cup of the parsley, 1 tsp. each of the rosemary, marjoram and thyme. Add salt, pepper and eggs. Mix thoroughly and shape into an oval. Place 2 bacon strips in center of a foil-lined baking sheet and place oval on strips. Top with remaining 3 bacon strips. Bake uncovered for 25 minutes. Add frozen vegetables and creamer potatoes. Sprinkle with remaining ¼ cup parsley and remaining rosemary, marjoram and thyme. Baste with pan juices. Bake for 25 minutes until meat and vegetables are cooked. Slice loaf, place on an oval serving platter surrounded by vegetables and serve.

THREE MEAL BEEF

Servings: 4

When time permits, preparing a large roast for future dinners is wise. This chuck roast stars as a roast with potatoes and vegetables, second as a soup with vegetables and pasta or rice, and third as the base for a well-seasoned wrap.

CLASSIC ROAST BEEF WITH VEGETABLES

1 blade chuck roast, 4½ lb.
½ cup dried, chopped onions
4 tsp. garlic powder
salt and pepper to taste
1 pkg. (24 oz.) frozen stew vegetables
1¼ cups water
3 tbs. flour
beef broth

In a slow cooker or Dutch oven, season roast with onions, garlic powder, salt and pepper and cover with frozen vegetables. Pour in ¾ cup of the water. Cover and cook on low heat for 5 to 8 hours until vegetables are soft and meat is very tender. Remove roast and divide into thirds. Keep ⅓ warm. Reserve 2 cups pan juices. Store this and other 2 pieces of roast in the refrigerator no longer than 4 days or freeze up to 4 months. Remove vegetables to warm bowl and set aside. Combine flour with remaining ½ cup water. Stir into reserved pan juices to thicken, adding beef broth, if necessary. Correct seasoning and strain into a gravy boat. Slice roast and serve with vegetables and gravy.

HEARTY BEEF-VEGETABLE SOUP

Servings: 4

1/3 recipe *Classic Roast Beef*, page 82
4 cups mixed chopped vegetables, or 2 pkg. (1 lb. each)
    frozen soup vegetables
2 small tomatoes, peeled and chopped
3 cups reserved meat juices
1 large cube beef bouillon
4 cups hot water
2 sprigs flat-leaf parsley, chopped
salt and pepper to taste
3 cups cooked rice or pasta

In a stockpot, combine roast, vegetables, tomatoes, meat juices, bouillon cube, water, parsley, salt and pepper. Simmer for 30 to 40 minutes for fresh vegetables, 15 to 20 minutes for frozen vegetables. Add rice or pasta before serving in deep soup bowls.

NOTE: For the vegetables, use carrots, potatoes, onions, celery, peas, beans or corn.

BEEF WRAPS WITH SPICY SALSA

Servings: 4

1 jar (16 oz.) chunky-style salsa
1 medium-sized red onion, chopped
1 clove garlic, chopped
1 tbs. chopped jalapeño pepper
1 medium avocado, peeled, pitted, chopped
1½ cups chopped fresh cilantro leaves, packed, plus more for garnish
salt to taste
⅓ recipe *Classic Roast Beef*, page 82
four 10-inch flour tortillas, warmed

In a small bowl, combine salsa, onion, garlic, pepper, avocado, cilantro and salt; set aside. Shred beef and spoon over each tortilla, leaving a 1½-inch border on all sides. Top each with reserved salsa mixture. Fold right and left edges of tortilla over filling; fold bottom edge up and roll up jelly-roll fashion. Garnish with additional cilantro.

RIBS AND KRAUT

Servings: 4

The stout flavor of this dish comes from browning the pork ribs with the onions and herbs before adding the other ingredients. Prepare this hearty dinner early in the day so its fragrant aroma will welcome your family home. Round out the meal with rye or pumpernickel bread, mixed pickles and spicy mustard.

1½ lb. country-style spare ribs
1 large onion, thinly sliced
2 tbs. chopped fresh sage
1 tbs. chopped fresh thyme
1 tbs. chopped fresh rosemary
salt and pepper to taste
1 tart apple, cut into wedges
6 medium potatoes, peeled and sliced into quarters
1 jar (1 qt.) crisp sauerkraut
1 pint (16 oz.) beer
1 tbs. caraway seeds
½ lb. old-fashioned deli franks (4-6 depending on size)

Heat broiler to 500°. In a large Dutch oven, brown ribs, onion, sage, thyme rosemary and salt and pepper for 20 minutes, turning once. Pour off all but ¼ cup drippings. Lower oven temperature to 325°. Add apple, potatoes, sauerkraut, beer and caraway seeds to Dutch oven, gently mixing ingredients with browned ribs. Cover tightly and bake for 1 hour, adding franks during last 10 minutes of cooking.

LAMB STEW PROVENÇAL

Servings: 6

Cold winter nights and warm fragrant stews are good companions. Home-cooked stews are more flavorful if prepared in advance, chilled and reheated before serving. Orange zest and Pernod add distinct French accents to this stew.

¼ cup extra virgin olive oil
2 medium onions, chopped
3 tsp. minced garlic
2½ lb. boneless lamb stew meat, cut into 1½-inch slices
6 medium carrots, peeled and cut into 3-inch-x-½-inch slices
3 tbs. orange peel (zest), plus more for garnish
1 tsp. dried thyme, crumbled
1 tsp. dried rosemary, crumbled
1 tsp. dried marjoram, crumbled
1 can (28 oz.) plum tomatoes with juice
1 cup dry white wine
2 tbs. Pernod or other anise-flavored liqueur
1 pkg. (10 oz.) frozen pearl onions, thawed
1 cup oil-cured black olives
salt and pepper to taste
fresh rosemary sprigs for garnish

Heat oven to 325°. In a 5-quart flameproof casserole, heat olive oil. Sauté onions and 2 tsp. of the garlic over medium-high heat until onions are soft. Add lamb, carrots, orange peel, thyme, rosemary and marjoram. Cook for 3 to 5 minutes, stirring frequently, until lamb loses its color and carrots begin to wilt. Combine tomatoes with wine and Pernod. Pour over lamb mixture and bring to a boil. Cover, place in oven and bake until lamb is tender, for about 1½ hours. Stir in pearl onions, black olives, remaining 1 tsp. minced garlic, salt and pepper. Bake for an additional 10 to 15 minutes, or until heated through. Garnish with fresh rosemary and orange peel.

VEGGIE BURGERS

Servings: 4

This Mediterranean-style burger rewards hungry appetites.

½ cup toasted almonds
¼ cup sunflower kernels
2 cups garbanzo beans, drained,
  3 tbs. liquid reserved
½ tsp. cumin
¼ tsp. ground cinnamon
3 cloves garlic, coarsely chopped
3 green onions, coarsely chopped
1 cup coarsely chopped mushrooms
1 tbs. extra virgin olive oil
1 egg, slightly beaten
salt and pepper to taste
½ cup sesame seeds
8 sesame seed buns

In a food processor workbowl, grind almonds and sunflower seeds to a coarse paste. Add garbanzos and bean liquid, cumin, allspice and cinnamon. Transfer to a bowl and set aside. Wipe workbowl clean and process garlic, onions and mushrooms. In a skillet, over medium-high heat, heat oil and sauté mushroom mixture until heated through, about 3 minutes. When cool, add to garbanzo mixture. Season with salt and pepper and mix well; fold in egg. Form 8 patties, coat with sesame seeds and place on a waxpaper-lined baking sheet. Refrigerate for 30 minutes, or until firm.

Grill patties on an oiled stove-top grill for 4 minutes on each side, or until brown. Serve on sesame seed buns.

FAST MEALS

SZECHWAN NOODLE SALAD

Servings: 4

Chinese sausage and Szechwan chili paste are available in Asian markets, but if they're not readily available, you can substitute fully-cooked smoked sausage and Tabasco Sauce. Enjoy with ice tea and almond cookies.

3 tbs. low-sodium soy sauce
3 tbs. rice vinegar
3 tbs. minced fresh ginger
2 tbs. sesame oil
2 tsp. sugar
1 tsp. salt
2 tbs. Szechwan chili paste
1 pkg. (12 oz.) fresh Chinese noodles
1 tbs. peanut oil
½ lb. cooked medium shrimp, cut into pieces
¼ lb. cooked Chinese sausage, cut into ½-inch slices
2 red bell peppers, stemmed, seeded and cut into ¼-inch strips
4 green onions, chopped
2 cups snow peas, blanched and cut into ¼-inch strips
3 cups bean sprouts, blanched
2 cups cilantro leaves

In a small dish, combine soy sauce, rice vinegar, ginger, sesame oil, sugar, salt and chili paste. Mix well and let stand for at least 1 hour. In a large pot, cook noodles in boiling water for 1 to 3 minutes. Drain and coat with oil. When cool, combine noodles with shrimp, sausage, peppers, onions, snow peas, bean sprouts and cilantro leaves. Add dressing to noodle mixture and serve.

VEGETABLE COUSCOUS SALAD

Servings: 4

A taste of Morocco travels to your supper table. Follow package directions when preparing the couscous, using broth instead of water for more flavor.

1 medium eggplant, cut into 1-inch cubes
2 medium zucchini, cut into 1-inch cubes
1 medium red bell pepper, stemmed, seeded and cut into 1-inch dice
4 medium tomatoes, quartered
1 bulb fennel, cut into 1-inch pieces
1 large red onion, cut into 1-inch slices
4 cloves garlic, slivered
1 cup shredded fresh basil leaves
1/4 cup extra virgin olive oil
salt and pepper to taste
2 pkg. (5.9 oz. each) couscous
vegetable broth
Cumin-Lime Dressing, follows
1/4 lb. mixed salad greens
6 oz. goat cheese, crumbled

Heat oven to 425°. In a large, shallow baking pan, add vegetables, garlic, basil, salt and pepper. Pour oil over and mix well. Roast for 20 to 30 minutes until vegetables are tender and brown around edges; set aside. Prepare couscous according to package directions, substituting vegetable broth for water. Set aside.

Servings: 4

CUMIN-LIME DRESSING

½ cup olive oil
¼ cup fresh lime juice
1 tsp. garlic powder
1 tsp. cayenne pepper
2 tsp. ground cumin
1 tsp. fennel seeds, crushed

In a small serving bowl, mix olive oil, lime juice, garlic powder, red pepper, cumin and fennel. On 4 plates, layer the salad greens, couscous, roasted vegetables and goat cheese. Pass dressing for drizzling.

ARTICHOKE PIE

Servings: 6

This savory dish is layered with the Provençal flavors of capers, anchovies and spices that make the artichoke paste or "tapenade". Look for artichoke tapenade in gourmet stores. Mellow fontina cheese enhances the sweetness of the artichokes.

one 9-inch frozen pie shell
2 pkg. (8 oz. each) frozen artichoke hearts, thawed
1/4 cup extra virgin olive oil
12 leeks, white parts only, sliced into rings
2 cloves garlic, minced
3/4 cup artichoke tapenade
4 eggs, lightly beaten
1/2 lb. fontina cheese, shredded
1/2 cup grated Asiago cheese
salt and pepper to taste

Heat oven to 450°. Thaw pie shell while preparing filling. Cut artichoke hearts into 1/2-inch wedges and set aside. Heat oil and sauté leeks and garlic for 3 minutes. Add artichoke hearts and cook for 3 minutes. Cool before stirring in tapenade, eggs, cheeses, salt and pepper. Pour into pie shell. Lower oven temperature to 425° and bake pie for 35 to 45 minutes until golden brown.

TAMALE PIE

Servings: 6

These flavors of the Southwest are straightforward enough for children, providing mild salsas are used. Corn on the cob or a simple onion, zucchini and tomato sauté completes the meal.

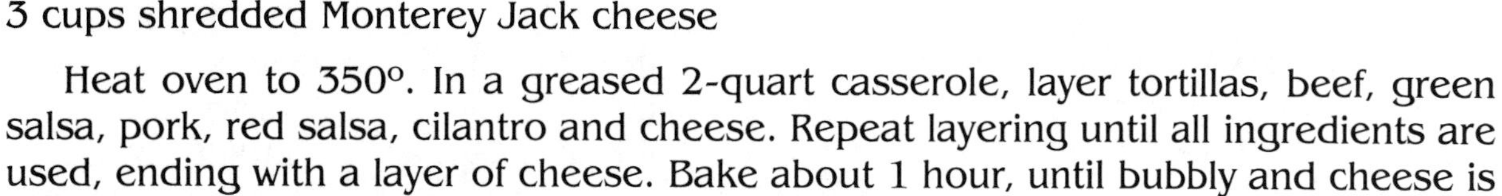

1 pkg. (13 oz.) corn tortillas
2 cups shredded cooked beef
2 cups mild green salsa
2 cups shredded cooked pork or chicken
2 cups mild red salsa
1 cup fresh cilantro leaves, optional
3 cups shredded Monterey Jack cheese

Heat oven to 350°. In a greased 2-quart casserole, layer tortillas, beef, green salsa, pork, red salsa, cilantro and cheese. Repeat layering until all ingredients are used, ending with a layer of cheese. Bake about 1 hour, until bubbly and cheese is lightly browned. Serve wedges directly from casserole dish.

ASPARAGUS FRITTATA

Servings: 4

Tender, thin asparagus are best in this frittata. Its simplicity and delicate taste make it a fine choice for an informal luncheon or a light family supper. For best results, cook the frittata slowly over low heat.

6 eggs
½ tsp. water
½ cup grated Parmesan cheese
salt and pepper to taste
¼ cup chopped fresh basil leaves
3 tbs. extra virgin olive oil
2 cloves garlic, thinly sliced
1 lb. pencil-thin asparagus, cut into ½-inch diagonal pieces
whole basil leaves for garnish,
sliced tomato for garnish

In a large bowl, lightly beat eggs with water until blended. Add cheese, salt, pepper and basil; set aside. In a large, nonstick skillet over high heat, stir-fry garlic and asparagus in 2 tbs. of the oil until asparagus is tender-crisp, about 2 minutes. Cover asparagus with egg mixture. Turn heat to low and add remaining 1 tbs. oil to skillet. Cook coated asparagus for about 15 minutes, or until eggs are set and creamy in center. Cover skillet with inverted plate and flip so frittata sits on plate. Slide frittata back into skillet and continue to cook for 2 minutes, until light brown on bottom. Slide onto a serving plate and cut into wedges. Top with basil leaves and sliced tomato.

HAM, MUSHROOM AND SPINACH FRITTATA

Servings: 4

Frittatas are versatile and economical. Combining basic ingredients with a few spices and herbs produces a laundry list of frittatas.

6 eggs
½ cup grated Parmesan cheese
2 tbs. chopped fresh flat-leaf parsley
2 tbs. chopped fresh sage
salt and white pepper to taste
3 tbs. extra virgin olive oil
¼ cup chopped green onions
1 cup diced cooked ham
⅓ cup sliced mushrooms
1 pkg. (10 oz.) frozen chopped spinach, thawed and squeezed dry

Heat broiler. In a bowl, lightly beat eggs until blended. Add cheese, parsley, sage, salt and pepper; set aside. Heat 2 tbs. of the oil in a large ovenproof nonstick skillet over medium heat. Sauté onions for 3 minutes, until soft. Add ham and mushrooms and continue cooking for 1 minute longer, or until mushrooms are soft. Transfer onion-ham mixture into bowl with eggs and add spinach. Turn heat to low and add remaining 1 tbs. oil. Pour in egg mixture, shaking skillet to evenly distribute ingredients. Cook for 15 minutes, until eggs are set, but creamy in center. Finish cooking under broiler, just until top is set 1 minute longer. Slide onto a serving platter and cut into wedges.

CALAMARI SANDWICHES

Servings: 4

Quickly fried calamari, spiced with chili powder, is sandwiched between slices of herbed focaccia bread. Cleaned calamari bodies and frozen focaccia should be available in most supermarkets. If not, shrimp or scallops and crusty French bread, split and sprinkled with olive oil and dried herbs, can be substituted.

1 cup flour
1 tsp. chili powder
salt and pepper to taste
2 lb. cleaned calamari bodies, cut into 1/4-inch rings
1 loaf herbed focaccia (1 1/2 lb.), quartered and sliced diagonally
canola or vegetable oil for frying
1/4 cup canola oil
1 tbs. Dijon-style mustard
salt and pepper to taste
4 cups baby salad greens
1 cup diced green and yellow zucchini
1 cup shaved Parmesan cheese
2 tbs. chopped fresh lemon peel (zest)

Mix flour, chili powder, salt and pepper in a paper bag. In batches, shake clean, dry calamari rings in flour mixture to lightly coat. Shake excess flour from calamari and place rings on a baking sheet. Let rest for 10 minutes. Place ½ focaccia slice on each of 4 plates; set aside. Heat oil in a large, deep saucepan until oil is hot, but not smoking. Cook calamari in small batches so each ring floats freely in oil. Cook briefly until goldenbrown and drain well on a stack of paper towels. In a medium bowl, whisk canola oil, mustard, salt and pepper until smooth. Toss salad greens, zucchini, Parmesan and lemon zest with dressing. Divide evenly and arrange on top of half foccacia. Top with cooked calamari. Cover with remaining half of focaccia to eat out of hand or eat open-faced with a fork and knife.

CALIFORNIA CANNELLONI

Servings: 4-6

California cooks know the short-cuts to classic cooking. Here, the cannelloni are actually won ton wrappers stuffed with Italian goodies.

2 cups cooked chopped spinach
8 green onions, chopped
3 tbs. chopped fresh flat-leaf parsley
10 oz. ricotta cheese
1 cup shredded Monterey Jack cheese
1 cup grated Parmesan cheese
18 won ton wrappers
3 cups tomato sauce
2 cups (17 oz.) prepared Alfredo sauce
1/4 cup chopped fresh oregano leaves

Heat oven to 350°. In a large bowl, mix spinach, onions, parsley, ricotta, Jack cheese and 1/2 cup of the Parmesan cheese. Spread an oiled, rectangular baking pan with 1 3/4 cups tomato sauce. Spoon filling in center of each won ton wrapper. Roll up and place seam-side down over tomato sauce, leaving space between won tons. Cover with Alfredo sauce. Pour in remaining 1 1/4 cups tomato sauce. Sprinkle with oregano and remaining 1/2 cup Parmesan. Bake for 45 minutes, or until heated through.

MEDITERRANEAN ROLL-UPS

Servings: 4

Armenian cracker bread dates back to Biblical times when Armenian families wrapped diced meats, vegetables and grains in the "cracker." Hummus, spiced garbanzo bean spread, is widely available in supermarkets and Middle Eastern markets.

1 pkg. soft cracker bread (2-4 sheets, depending on size)
1/4 lb. whipped cream cheese
1/4 lb. hummus
2 cups baby spinach leaves
1/2 cup chopped kalamata olives
1 cup drained, thinly sliced marinated artichoke hearts
1/4 cup thinly sliced roasted red bell peppers
1/2 cup crumbled feta cheese

Place all ingredients in separate piles on sheets of wax paper. Cover each bread with a layer of cream cheese. Spread hummus over 3/4 of the cream cheese, leaving 4-inches of one end uncovered. This end will seal the roll. Arrange spinach leaves over hummus and sprinkle olives, artichoke hearts, peppers and cheese over spinach leaves. Tightly roll bread toward exposed cream cheese end. Place rolls in plastic bags and refrigerate for about 10 minutes before slicing into 1½-inch pinwheels. Secure with toothpicks and serve.

SMOKED TURKEY AND JACK ROLL-UPS

Servings: 4

Roll-ups can also make colorful hors d'oeuvres when cut into pinwheels and served on a bed of watercress with black and green olives.

1/4 lb. whipped cream cheese
1/4 cup mango chutney
1 1/2 tsp. finely chopped fresh tarragon
4 sheets soft cracker bread
1 cup packed watercress leaves
1/2 lb. Monterey Jack cheese, thinly sliced
1/2 lb. smoked turkey, thinly sliced
1 small red onion, thinly sliced
1/4 cup toasted and chopped almonds

In a small bowl, blend cream cheese, chutney and tarragon until smooth. Spread in a thin layer on each cracker bread. Cover with watercress, leaving 1/4 of the cream cheese layer exposed on one end. This end will seal the roll. Layer Jack cheese over watercress, followed by another layer of cream cheese and watercress and a layer of smoked turkey. Repeat layering, ending with layer of onion and almonds. Tightly roll toward exposed cream cheese mixture end. Chill roll-ups in a plastic bag until ready to serve; cut into 1 1/2-inch pinwheel slices.

GRILLED PACIFIC RIM SWORDFISH

Servings: 4

Versatile swordfish shines when it is bathed in a peppery marinade, grilled and served over fresh vegetables and salad greens.

4 fresh or frozen, swordfish steaks
1/4 cup lime juice
2 tbs. dry white wine
2 tbs. vegetable oil
1 tsp. sesame oil
1 tbs. low-sodium soy sauce
6 cups mixed baby greens
3/4 cup thinly sliced radishes
1 green Anaheim chile pepper, stemmed, seeded and chopped
lime slices

Prepare medium-hot barbecue.

Dry fresh fish on paper towels; thaw and dry fish, if frozen. Place in a plastic bag with lime juice, wine, oils and soy sauce. Seal and refrigerate for 6 hours, turning bag occasionally. In a large bowl, mix greens, radishes and chile pepper. Divide evenly among 4 salad plates. Drain fish, reserving marinade in a small saucepan.

Grill fish in grill basket directly over medium-hot coals for 8 to 12 minutes, depending on size and thickness. Heat reserved marinade on grill until boiling for food safety purposes. Top greens with swordfish and lime slices and drizzle with marinade.

RED SNAPPER WITH TEN HERBS

Servings: 4

Economical red snapper is quickly sautéed with fresh and dried herbs and tossed with farfalle (bowtie) pasta. Surprisingly, the herbs do not compete for flavor; rather, they blend well to flavor this normally mild fish. If farfalle is not available, choose another small pasta with open cavities that will catch the sauce.

1 lb. farfalle
1½ lb. red snapper fillets, cut into 1-inch diagonal pieces
2 tbs. dried chervil
2 tbs. dried marjoram
2 tbs. dried sage
2 tbs. dried tarragon
1 tbs. dried oregano
1 tbs. rosemary
1 tbs. thyme
3 tbs. chopped fresh basil
3 tbs. chopped fresh flat-leaf parsley
2 tbs. chopped fresh chives
salt and pepper to taste
½ cup extra virgin olive oil, plus more if needed
3 cloves garlic, minced
½ tsp. red pepper flakes
freshly ground black peper
freshly grated Parmesan cheese, optional

Cook farfalle in a large pot of rapidly boiling salted water until slightly firm to the bite, *al dente*, about 3 minutes. Drain pasta, reserving 1/4 cup cooking water, and place in a warm bowl.

In a large ceramic bowl, combine red snapper with ten herbs, salt, pepper and 1/4 cup of the olive oil. Mix well and set aside. Heat a large skillet over medium-high heat and add 2 tbs. of the oil. Gently sauté garlic and red pepper flakes until aromatic. In two batches, cook red snapper and herb mixture with garlic and red pepper for 3 minutes, shaking skillet constantly and adding more oil, if necessary. Fish should be brown around edges and opaque inside. Remove from skillet and keep warm. Repeat with second batch. Return cooked snapper and cooked farfalle to skillet. Fold gently so fish, herbs and pasta are well mixed, adding reserved pasta cooking water if too dry. Serve immediately with a few grindings of pepper and sprinkle with Parmesan cheese, if desired.

CALAMARI COUSCOUS

Servings: 4

The flavor of the sea comes from the shrimp bouillon that is dissolved in the couscous. Shrimp bouillon cubes are available at most Asian markets. Reconstitute and use them as a flavor booster in other fish and seafood dishes or as a substitute for clam juice. Calamari bodies are available fresh or frozen at the seafood counter in most food markets.

1 shrimp bouillon cube, dissolved in 2½ cups boiling water
2 cups instant couscous
¾ cup extra virgin olive oil
2 tbs. lemon juice
1 clove garlic, minced
½ cup chopped fresh basil
salt and pepper to taste
20 calamari bodies, cut into ¼-inch rings
1 cucumber, peeled and sliced ¼-inch thick
2 cups small cherry tomatoes
1 cup dry-cured Moroccan olives
16 outer leaves radicchio
whole basil leaves for garnish
lemon wedges for garnish

In a large bowl, pour shrimp bouillon over couscous. Cover and let stand for 10 minutes until bouillon is absorbed; fluff grains with a fork. In a second bowl, whisk lemon juice with oil, garlic, basil, salt and pepper. Fold in calamari, cucumber, tomatoes and olives. Arrange radicchio on chilled plates. Mound couscous on radicchio and top with calamari mixture. Garnish with basil leaves and lemon wedges.

SPICY TOFU WRAPS

Servings: 4

A warm flour tortilla spiked with sesame oil makes an unusual holder for this spicy Asian-inspired filling.

3 tsp. cornstarch
1/4 cup soy sauce
3 tbs. cider vinegar
3 cloves garlic, minced
3 tbs. chopped fresh cilantro
1/2 tsp. red pepper flakes
2 tsp. sesame oil
6 large flour tortillas
3 tbs. peanut oil
1 medium onion, thinly sliced
1 cup thinly sliced celery
1 1/2 cups broccoli florets
2 cups thinly sliced mushrooms
3 cups cubed firm tofu
1 1/2 cups bean sprouts
1/2 cup sliced almonds
hoisin sauce, optional

In a small bowl, whisk cornstarch, soy sauce and vinegar. Add garlic, cilantro and pepper flakes. Mix well and set aside. Heat oven to 350°. Dab sesame oil on each tortilla and stack in damp paper towel. Wrap stack in foil and bake until warm, about 10 minutes. Heat peanut oil over high heat in a wok or large skillet. Add onion and celery. Stir-fry for 3 minutes until tender-crisp. Add broccoli and stir-fry for 2 more minutes. Add mushrooms and cook until mushrooms are soft. Lower heat, add tofu and toss until heated through. Stir in soy mixture, bean sprouts and almonds. Spoon equal amounts of filling in center of each tortilla, roll up and eat out of hand.

ROASTED CHICKEN AND VEGETABLES

Servings: 4

Three steps and you have dinner in the oven! For those times when a comforting meal is needed, this one can't be beat. Serve with soft buns and a simple salad of mixed greens and tomatoes.

3 lb. chicken pieces
1 tsp. salt
½ tsp. pepper
2 tbs. chopped fresh flat-leaf parsley
2 tbs. chopped fresh rosemary,
  or ½ tsp. dried
2 cloves garlic, minced
1 onion, thinly sliced
4 medium carrots, peeled and
  sliced ¼-inch thick
4 medium potatoes, peeled and
  sliced ¼-inch thick
2 tbs. extra virgin olive oil
½ cup dry white wine

Heat broiler to 500°. Season chicken with salt and pepper. Place in a large, shallow baking pan and brown for about 8 minutes, turning once. Remove pan and reduce oven temperature to 350°. Add parsley, rosemary, garlic, onion, carrots, potatoes, olive oil and wine to chicken. Cover pan with foil. Bake for 1 hour until vegetables are barely tender. Remove foil and bake for ½ hour, until chicken is golden brown.

SWEET AND SOUR CHICKEN

Servings: 4

Fusion flavors are served over a nest of jasmine rice. Have almond cookies and sliced oranges on hand to satisfy the dessert craving.

1 cup pitted California green olives
3/4 cup extra virgin olive oil
3 tbs. red wine vinegar
peel (zest) of 2 oranges, grated
peel (zest) of 1 lemon, grated
4 cloves garlic, sliced
pinch red pepper flakes
8 large skinned and boned chicken thighs
1 large onion, chopped
2 cloves garlic, minced
2 cups diagonally cut fresh asparagus pieces, 1/2-inch pieces
3 tbs. fresh oregano leaves
1 tsp. ground cumin
2 tbs. balsamic vinegar
salt and pepper to taste
4 cups hot cooked jasmine rice
2 tbs. chopped fresh flat-leaf parsley

In a bowl, combine olives, ½ cup of the oil, vinegar, citrus zest, garlic, pepper flakes and chicken. Refrigerate for 2 hours, stirring twice. In a skillet over medium heat, cook onion in remaining ¼ cup oil for 3 minutes. Add garlic and asparagus. Cook for 4 to 5 minutes, until onion is translucent. Remove from pan and set aside. In same pan, brown drained chicken and season with oregano and cumin. Return vegetables to skillet and add marinade. Cover and cook over low heat for 30 to 35 minutes, until chicken is tender. Stir in balsamic vinegar, salt and pepper. Serve over rice and sprinkle with parsley.

DELICATA SQUASH RISOTTO

Servings: 4

With a bounty of fall and winter vegetables, risotto becomes the perfect vehicle to showcase these flavors. Rich delicata squash tastes of sweet potato and butternut squash. Splurge and drizzle each serving with white truffle oil.

3 tsp. unsalted butter
1 tsp. extra virgin olive oil
1 large onion, minced
1 cup tiny cubes delicata squash
1½ cups Arborio rice
½ cup dry white wine
4½ cups hot chicken or vegetable broth
½ cup grated Parmesan cheese
1 tbs. minced flat-leaf parsley
1 tbs. minced sage
truffle oil for drizzling, optional

In a heavy 2½-quart saucepan over low heat, melt butter and add oil. Cook onion until soft, about 10 minutes. Add squash and cook until tender. Raise heat to high and stir in rice. Coat with butter and squash mixture. When rice is heated through, add wine and stir constantly until absorbed. Add broth in ½-cup intervals, stirring constantly until absorbed and adding until all broth is used, mixture becomes creamy and rice is cooked. Remove from heat and season with cheese and herbs. Mix well. Cover and allow to stand 3 minutes. Divide risotto among 4 bowls. Top each with truffle oil, if desired.

STIR-FRIED WILD RICE AND BEEF

Servings: 4

The nutty flavor and chewiness of wild rice adds texture to this stir-fry. Wild rice is not rice at all, but a long-grain marsh grass.

1 cup wild rice
1 can (10.5 oz.) beef broth, defatted
2¾ cups water
1 lb. beef tenderloin, sliced crosswise into thin strips
¼ cup peanut oil
2 cloves garlic, minced
4 green onions, chopped
¾ cup broccoli florets and chopped tender stems
¾ cup sliced mushrooms
½ cup cherry tomatoes
2 tbs. low-sodium soy sauce
2 tbs. dry sherry

Combine rice, broth and water. Cover and cook over low heat on top of stove for 45 minutes, until tender, or in rice cooker until done. In a wok or large skillet, stir-fry beef in hot oil for about 2 minutes, until brown. Remove and set aside. In same pan, stir-fry garlic, onions, broccoli, mushrooms and tomatoes for about 1 or 2 minutes until tender-crisp. Stir in rice, beef and accumulated juices, soy sauce and sherry. Heat through and serve.

JAPANESE PORK AND EGGPLANT

Servings: 4

Shoyu, miso and sake impart an Asian flavor to tender pork slices and Japanese eggplant. Stir-fry briefly cooked udon to complete this spicy dish. If udon, flat, wide Japanese noodles are not readily available, fresh fettuccine will do.

1 bag (14 oz.) fresh udon or fresh fettuccini
6 tbs. peanut oil
2 cloves garlic, crushed
½-inch piece fresh ginger, coarsely chopped
1 Anaheim chile, stemmed and seeded
½ lb. pork tenderloin, thinly sliced
5 Japanese eggplants, diagonally sliced
2 red bell peppers, stemmed, seeded and thinly sliced
2 green onions, sliced diagonally
¼ cup shoyu (Japanese soy sauce) or light soy sauce
¼ cup brown sugar, packed
¼ cup miso (fermented soy bean paste)
3 tbs. sake (Japanese rice wine) or sherry
½ cup chopped walnuts, toasted
chopped fresh cilantro for garnish

Cook udon in a large pot of rapidly boiling salted water until slightly firm to the bite, *al dente*, about 3 minutes. Drain pasta, leaving a little water clinging to it, and place in a warm bowl.

In a large skillet or wok, heat 2 tbs. of the oil over medium-high heat. Stir-fry garlic, ginger and chile pepper for 2 minutes; discard. Return skillet to heat. Add 2 tbs. oil and stir-fry pork until brown. Lower heat to medium. Add remaining 2 tbs. oil and eggplant to skillet. Cook covered for about 8 minutes, until eggplant is barely tender. In a small bowl, whisk together shoyu, sugar, miso and sake. Stir in peppers, onion and shoyu mixture. Cover and cook for about 4 minutes, until liquid is almost evaporated. Stir in udon and walnuts. Serve on heated platters and garnish with cilantro.

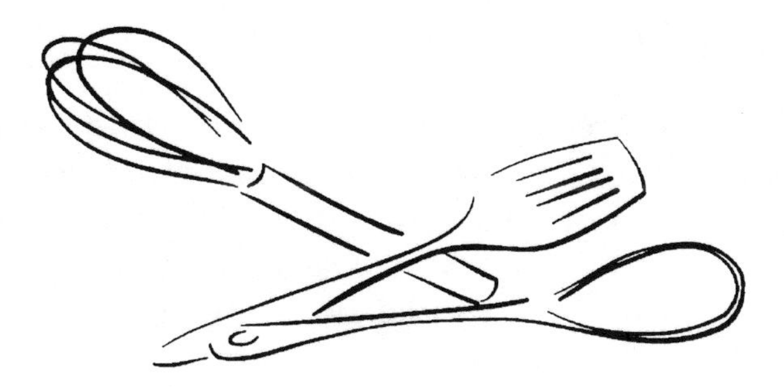

CHICKEN CURRY PITAS

Servings: 4

Curry powder, the signature flavor of Indian cooking, is a blend of 20 herbs, spices and seeds. Authentic Indian curry powder is ground daily; thus the taste varies with the cook and the region. Use curry powder to brighten leftover chicken, rice and crisp vegetables.

3 cups diced cooked chicken
2 cups cooked rice
1 cup finely chopped celery
1/2 cup chopped mixed green and red sweet peppers
1/4 cup chopped green onions
1/2 cup chopped, toasted almonds
2 tsp. curry powder
1/4 tsp. celery seeds
1 1/2 tsp. lemon juice
1/2 cup nonfat cottage cheese
1/4 cup nonfat plain yogurt
salt and pepper to taste
4 pita breads, cut in half

In a large bowl, combine chicken, rice, celery, peppers, onions and almonds. Mix well. In a heavy skillet over medium heat, toast curry powder for 3 minutes, until aromatic; cool. In a food processor workbowl, place celery seeds, lemon juice, cottage cheese and yogurt. Add curry and process until liquefied. Season with salt and pepper. Pour dressing over chicken mixture and divide chicken mixture evenly into pita pockets.

SPRING VEGETABLE STEW

Servings: 4

The first picking of home-grown vegetables anticipates the bounty of summer. Enjoy a marvelous stew made just for the harvest. A mild Greek feta cheese, a loaf of crusty French bread and a bottle of light white wine complete this meal.

3 tbs. lemon juice
4-6 medium artichokes
¼ cup extra virgin olive oil
8 green garlic bulbs and stalks (about 1 cup), chopped
4 cloves garlic, chopped
1 bulb fennel and greens, chopped
2 cups shelled fava beans
1 cup vegetable broth
2 tbs. chopped fresh thyme
1 tbs. chopped fresh mint
salt and pepper to taste

Fill a large bowl with water and add lemon juice. Prepare artichokes by removing stems and tough outer leaves, stopping when tender yellow leaves are reached. Cut ⅓ from top and discard. Quarter artichokes and remove thistles and chokes. Cut into eighths and drop into water. In a large skillet, heat olive oil over medium-high heat. Sauté artichokes for 5 minutes and add garlic, fennel and fava beans. Cook for 10 minutes, until vegetables brown slightly. Add broth and seasoning and stir well. Cover and simmer for 20 minutes, until artichokes are tender.

VEGETABLE AND CRAB FRIED RICE

Servings: 4

Precooked chilled rice is added to stir-fried, seasoned vegetables of your choice and marinated crabmeat to produce a quick dinner. Look for the unfamiliar ingredients in Asian markets or the Asian section of most food markets.

1/4 cup minced garlic
2 1/2 tbs. minced fresh ginger
1 tsp. Chinese five-spice powder
3 tbs. low-sodium soy sauce
1/4 cup sake (Japanese rice wine)
1/4 cup chicken broth
1 lb. crabmeat, rinsed and flaked
3 tbs. peanut oil
1/2 cup chopped green onions, white part only
1 cup red bell pepper strips
2 cups thinly sliced mixed vegetables, such as peas, carrots, corn and potatoes or thawed frozen mixed vegetable cubes
4 cups thinly sliced mushrooms
5 cups cooked rice
3 tbs. mirin (Japanese rice wine)
1 cup chopped fresh chives

In a medium bowl, mix 2 tbs. of the garlic, 1½ tbs. of the ginger, five-spice powder, 2 tbs. of the soy sauce, sake and 2 tbs. of the chicken broth. Add crab pieces and stir gently to coat pieces with marinade; set aside. In a wok or large skillet, heat 1 tbs. of the oil and stir-fry remaining 2 tbs. garlic and 1 tbs. ginger with green onions and bell pepper for 2 minutes, until fragrant, brightly colored and tender-crisp. Remove to bowl and set aside. Stir-fry vegetables for 2 minutes and add to bowl. Add remaining 2 tbs. oil and stir-fry mushrooms for 3 minutes. Return vegetables to pan with crab, marinade and rice. Heat through, stirring constantly for 1½ to 2 minutes. Stir in remaining 2 tbs. chicken broth, mirin and chives. Serve immediately.

ABRUZZO-STYLE VEGETABLE MELANGE

Servings: 6-8

Based on a recipe from Abruzzo, Italy, this melange of vegetables is paired with medium seashell-shaped pasta for a quick-fix supper. Serve with bread and white wine. Chilled melon and a semisoft goat cheese bring the meal to a close.

1 large red onion, thinly sliced
1 stalk celery with leaves, thinly sliced
2 large carrots, thinly sliced
1 large baking potato, peeled and thinly sliced
2 medium yellow zucchini, thinly sliced
2 medium green zucchini, thinly sliced
1 red bell pepper, stemmed, seeded and thinly sliced
1 cup sliced green beans
2 large extra-ripe tomatoes, crushed
2 tbs. extra virgin olive oil
1/4 cup chopped fresh basil
1/4 cup chopped fresh flat-leaf parsley
2 cups medium-sized sea shell pasta
1 can (8 oz.) tomato sauce
2 cups cold water
salt and pepper to taste

In a large Dutch oven, combine vegetables, oil, herbs and pasta. Add tomato sauce and cold water and mix well. Bring to a boil, reduce heat and simmer, covered, for 50 minutes, stirring occasionally, until vegetables and pasta are tender and liquid is nearly evaporated. Check stew after 20 minutes. Add more liquid, if necessary. Serve in soup bowls and season with salt and pepper.

SUPERFAST MEALS

DANDELION GREENS WITH NUTS AND RICOTTA

Servings: 4

Dandelion greens are available year 'round in the produce section of most food markets. The slightly bitter, tart flavor is pleasing with creamy ricotta cheese and buttery nuts. Chai spice tea from India and warm cornbread make this an interesting lunch.

2 large bunches dandelion greens, leaves only
1 clove garlic
1/4 cup extra virgin olive oil
2 cups mixed raw nuts and seeds (filberts, cashews, almonds, sunflower seeds, and/or soy nuts)
2 cups ricotta cheese
paprika to taste

Microwave covered greens on HIGH for 4 minutes or steam until tender. Rub bottom of a large glass bowl with cut garlic clove; discard clove. Add cooked greens and olive oil and mix well. Divide greens among 4 plates and top with nut mixture. Around the perimeter of each plate, drop spoonfuls of ricotta. Serve with a sprinkling of paprika.

GREEK SPINACH SALAD

Servings: 4

A highly nutritious combination of iron-rich spinach and healthful soy beans provides abundant energy for the rest of the day. The color contrast and crunch of the dry-roasted soybeans add sensory appeal as well.

¼ cup extra virgin olive oil
2 tbs. coarse grain Dijon-style mustard
juice of ½ lemon
salt and pepper to taste
4 tomatoes, cut into 1-inch wedges
3 cups sliced mushrooms
10 cups washed spinach leaves
1 lb. feta cheese, crumbled
2 cups dry-roasted soy beans

In a large salad bowl, whisk olive oil with mustard, lemon juice, salt and pepper. Add tomatoes, mushrooms and spinach. Mix gently, but thoroughly. Top with feta cheese and soy beans.

FIG AND GORGONZOLA SALAD

Servings: 4

Grilling figs caramelizes the sugars, intensifying their sweetness. If you don't have time to grill, the salad is perfectly delicious with fully ripened figs.

5 tbs. walnut oil
1½ tsp. balsamic vinegar
salt and pepper to taste
9 cups salad greens, such as arugula or watercress
1 large red onion, thinly sliced
2 cups crumbled Gorgonzola cheese
2 cups walnut pieces, toasted
12 figs

In a large bowl, whisk oil, vinegar, salt and pepper. Add greens and onion slices and toss. Divide among 4 plates and sprinkle each with cheese and walnuts.

Prepare a medium-hot grill.

Cut figs in half lengthwise and thread on skewers making sure fruit lies flat. Brush with olive oil and grill 4-inches above medium-hot coals for 4 to 6 minutes, turning frequently, until hot and streaked with brown. Arrange 4 fig pieces on each plate.

WHITE BEAN SALAD

Servings: 2

Italians have a way of turning whatever is in the pantry into a substantial lunch or dinner. Here, canned cannellini beans, or white kidney beans, are combined with red onions, tomatoes and olive oil for a quick, satisfying lunch. Serve some imported provolone cheese and country bread as accompaniments.

¼ cup extra virgin olive oil
salt and pepper to taste
1 tbs. chopped fresh sage leaves
1 can (15 oz.) cannellini beans, rinsed and drained
4 Roma tomatoes, cut into wedges
1 medium-sized red onion, thinly sliced
6 cups torn endive or romaine leaves
5 oz. provolone cheese, cut into wedges
crusty bread

In a large salad bowl, whisk oil, salt, pepper and sage. Add beans, tomatoes, onion and endive. Mix gently, taking care not to crush beans. Serve immediately with wedges of provolone cheese and bread.

SARDINES AND GREENS

Servings: 4

Serving a salad supper once a week is a fine way to keep healthy. This salad is particularly rich in calcium, since one large serving of canned sardines with edible bones contains nearly 500 mg. Look for canned sardines from Morocco. Packed in soy oil, they are more flavorful than sardines from Norway. This satisfying salad can be made with any combination of fresh vegetables and greens. Serve with a multi-grain country bread and rice pudding for dessert.

1/4 cup canola oil
2 tbs. Dijon-style mustard
juice of 1 lemon or lime
salt and pepper to taste
2 cups cauliflower florets and tender chopped stems
1 cup sliced red bell pepper
1 cup peeled, sliced cucumber
1 cup sliced radishes
1 cup peas
2 cans (125 g each) oil-packed sardines
6 cups mixed salad greens (romaine, garden lettuce and endive)
1/2 cup chopped fresh flat-leaf parsley

In a large salad bowl, combine oil, mustard, lemon or lime juice, salt and pepper; mix well. Add vegetables and sardines with oil. Fold in greens, coating all leaves with dressing. When ingredients are blended, top with chopped parsley.

TANDOORI CHICKEN SALAD

Servings: 4

Eclectic dishes that sport contrasting tastes, textures and temperatures usually confuse the palate. This is not the case with this straightforward salad that blends flavors from India, Asia and Europe.

1 small tomato, peeled and chopped
2 cloves garlic, minced
2 tbs. chopped fresh cilantro leaves
3/4 cup extra virgin olive oil
1/4 cup balsamic vinegar
salt and pepper to taste
1 medium-sized red onion, thinly sliced
2 cups mixed red and yellow cherry tomatoes
1 cup pitted kalamata olives
3 cups cubed *Tandoori Chicken*, page 60, 1 1/2-inch cubes
1/2 lb. fresh mozzarella cheese, drained and cut into 1/2-inch slices
6 cups mixed salad greens
1 cup fresh cilantro leaves
1 cup alfalfa sprouts
freshly grated Parmesan cheese

In a large salad bowl, whisk together tomato, garlic, cilantro, oil, vinegar, salt and pepper. Mix in onion, cherry tomatoes, olives, chicken and cheese. Fold in salad greens, cilantro and alfalfa sprouts. Divide among 4 chilled salad plates and pass the Parmesan cheese around the table.

GRILLED CHICKEN SALAD

Servings: 4

For this dinner, salad greens are dressed up with substantial flavor. A stove-top grill cooks the chicken quickly.

1/4 cup olive oil
1 1/2 tbs. balsamic vinegar
1 1/2 tsp. minced garlic
salt and pepper to a taste
4 chicken breasts, skinned and boned
6 cups baby salad greens
1 cup torn romaine lettuce
1 cup crumbled Gorgonzola cheese
1 cup walnut pieces, toasted

In a large bowl, mix 2 tbs. of the olive oil, 1/2 tsp. of the balsamic vinegar, 1 tsp. of the garlic, salt and pepper. Marinate chicken breasts in mixture for 2 hours in the refrigerator. Remove and wipe dry.

Prepare a medium-hot barbecue and cook chicken breasts for 7 to 8 minutes, until brown. Turn chicken and grill for 10 more minutes. Check for doneness by poking thickest part of chicken with a knife point. Meat should be opaque and juices clear. Remove from grill.

Slice chicken into ½-inch thick slices and set aside on a plate. In a large salad bowl, whisk together remaining 2 tbs. oil, 1 tbs. balsamic vinegar, 1 tsp. garlic, salt and pepper. Add greens and toss until well coated with dressing. Divide greens among 4 chilled plates. Arrange chicken slices over greens and top with cheese and walnut pieces.

GARDEN PEA SHOOT SALAD

Servings: 4

Asian flavors are accented in this crunchy salad. Bunches of pea shoots, the topmost leaves and tendrils of the snow pea plant, are available at Asian markets as well as local farmers' markets.

2 tbs. light soy sauce
1 tbs. rice vinegar
2 tsp. sesame oil
1/4 cup peanut oil
2 cups shelled fresh peas or thawed frozen peas
1 bunch baby radishes, cut into 1/4-inch slices
3 tsp. chopped fresh chives
2 bunches snow pea shoots or tender pea leaves,
  torn into bite-size pieces (about 8 cups)
1 cup bean sprouts
1/4 cup sesame seeds, toasted

In a large salad bowl, whisk soy sauce, vinegar and oils. Add peas, radishes and chives; mix well. Fold in pea shoots and sprouts. Top with sesame seeds. Serve immediately.

FIG AND ANCHOVY SALAD

Servings: 4

Presented on a bed of escarole, endive and arugula and accented with slices of vine-ripened tomatoes, this sweet and salty combination will grow on you. Serve with warm bread and fruity red wine for a taste of sunny Italy.

8 cups bite-sized pieces escarole, curly endive and arugula
8 large fresh figs, sliced
2 cans (2 oz. each) anchovy fillets, drained
3 large, firm tomatoes, sliced
12 kalamata olives, optional
extra virgin olive oil for drizzling
black pepper to taste

Divide greens among 4 plates. Arrange figs, tomato slices and anchovies on greens. Arrange olives on top of greens, if using. Drizzle oil over salad and sprinkle with black pepper.

MEDITERRANEAN MUSSEL SOUP

Servings: 4

The flavor of farm-raised mussels mimics that of the large, flavorful ones of the Mediterranean and they boast being virtually "beardless" and sand-free. A light scraping with a sharp knife quickly removes any black hairs that might peak through the shells. Humble vegetables, herbs, white wine and butter produce a soup that is tasteful. But, the meal isn't complete without a loaf of French bread.

4 lb. mussels, scrubbed and scraped
2 cups chopped leeks
1 cup diced tomatoes
2 cloves garlic, minced
2 tbs. fresh thyme leaves
2½ cups dry white wine
¼ lb. unsalted butter
salt and pepper to taste
juice of 1 lemon
1 cup chopped fresh flat-leaf parsley

In a large skillet, combine mussels, leeks, tomatoes, garlic, thyme and wine. Cover and cook over high heat for 5 or 6 minutes, shaking pan occasionally. Remove mussels as soon as they open, discarding half of each shell. Arrange mussels in warm soup bowls. Add butter, salt, pepper and lemon juice to liquid in pan. Boil rapidly, stirring constantly, until liquid is reduced by 1/3. Pour over mussels, sprinkle with parsley and serve at once.

YEAR 'ROUND CHICKEN SOUP

Servings: 4

A homestyle chicken soup can be made using canned chicken broth as a base, microwaving chicken breasts and vegetables, combining ingredients and simmering for a short time. From cupboard to table should take no more than 30 minutes. Keep the recipe on hand during cold and flu season.

2 chicken breast halves, skinned and boned
2 large carrots, peeled and thinly sliced
2 stalks celery with leaves, thinly sliced
1 qt. can (32 oz.) chicken broth
2 cups water
1 tbs. chopped fresh ginger
2 cloves garlic, minced
2 fresh flat-leaf parsley sprigs
salt and pepper to taste
4 cups cooked rice or tiny macaroni
freshly grated Parmesan cheese

Place chicken breasts on a platter with thicker ends towards outside edge of platter. Cover with plastic wrap. Microwave on HIGH for 8 minutes, turning once; set aside, reserving cooking liquid. Place carrots and celery one layer deep on platter. Cover and microwave on HIGH for 3 to 5 minutes; set aside, reserving cooking liquid. Cut chicken into pieces. In a large saucepan over medium heat, combine broth, water, ginger, garlic, parsley, salt, pepper, chicken, vegetables and cooking liquid from both chicken and vegetables. Bring to a boil and simmer for 10 minutes. Serve over rice with grated cheese.

COLD TOMATO-VEGETABLE SOUP

Servings: 8

Creamy, cold soups are particularly refreshing on hot summer days. Buttermilk or yogurt is the base for this soup, but buttermilk yields a milder taste than yogurt.

1 can (14.5 oz.) diced tomatoes with juice
1/4 cup chopped onion
2 1/2 cups buttermilk
1 tsp. salt
1 cup sliced white mushrooms
1 cup halved cherry tomatoes
1 cup fresh corn kernels
1/2 cup chopped green onions
1/2 cup chopped fresh cilantro
1/2 cup chopped fresh basil
chopped fresh flat-leaf parsley for garnish

In a food processor workbowl or blender container, puree canned tomatoes, onion, buttermilk and salt until smooth. Transfer to a serving bowl. Stir in mushrooms, tomatoes, corn, green onions, cilantro and basil. Serve very cold. Garnish with parsley. This soup can also be served hot in a chafing dish, or in a baking dish on an electric warming tray.

COLD CUCUMBER SOUP

Servings: 4

This delighful warm weather soup is best paired with large hunks of sourdough bread.

2 cucumbers, peeled and seeded
2 cloves garlic, chopped
2½ cups nonfat plain yogurt
2 tbs. vegetable oil
½ tsp. salt
½ cup chopped walnuts
½ cup chopped green onions
¼ cup chopped fresh mint

Grate 1 cucumber into a serving bowl; set aside. In a food processor workbowl, process remaining cucumber, garlic, yogurt, oil and salt until smooth. Pour into serving bowl with grated cucumber. Add walnuts, green onions and mint. Chill and serve.

CHILLED SHRIMP AND TOFU SOUP

Serves 4-6

This soup is a visual delight with colorful vegetable bits, tiny shrimp and rosy-hued tofu floating in a spicy tomato broth. This no-cooker can be assembled in less than 20 minutes the night before serving.

½ cup peeled, seeded, chopped cucumber
1 medium avocado, diced
1 small tomato, diced
¼ cup chopped red bell pepper
¼ cup fresh peas
½ lb. cooked tiny shrimp
¾ cup cubed firm tofu, 1-inch cubes
2 large cloves garlic, minced
1 small onion, finely chopped
1 qt. Clamato juice
1 tbs. sherry vinegar
2 tsp. balsamic vinegar
1 tbs. extra virgin olive oil
1 tsp. sugar
cayenne pepper to taste
1 tbs. chopped fresh lemon peel (zest)
1 cup fresh cilantro leaves

Place all ingredients in a large serving bowl and mix well. Cover and refrigerate overnight to give flavors the opportunity to combine. Serve in shallow soup bowls.

SEARED GARLIC STEAK SANDWICHES

Servings: 4

Similar in taste to the French dip sandwich, here, thin slices of rib steak are pan-fried. Partially freeze steak for ease in cutting. Purchase concentrated demi-glace in the canned soup section of food markets.

2 tbs. demi-glace
3/4 cup warm water
1/2 cup fat trimmings, or 1/2 cup extra-virgin olive oil
1 1/2 lb. rib steak, cut into 1/8-inch slices
4 cloves garlic, mashed
salt and pepper to taste
4 large French rolls
kosher dill pickles

In a small saucepan over medium-high heat, mix demi-glace with water. Bring to a boil, stirring constantly, and cook until creamy; set aside. In a large skillet, render fat from trimmings. Brown garlic in fat; remove garlic and discard. Quickly sauté beef slices in two batches; remove and keep warm. Scrape any brown bits from bottom of pan with reserved demi-glace. Bring to a boil. Lower heat to medium and simmer, returning cooked steak to pan for 1 minute to heat through. Split rolls horizontally and arrange beef and gravy on one side of each roll. Top with other half of roll and serve with pickle spears.

CRAB QUESADILLAS WITH CITRUS

Servings: 2

Think of quesadillas as grilled sandwiches from Mexico. Flour tortillas become the "bread," with delicious fillings folded inside. Quesadillas vary in color, texture and flavor. Enjoy them with a glass of Mexican beer or frosty limeade.

1 cup shredded Swiss cheese
1 tbs. cream cheese, softened
1 tsp. orange juice
1 tsp. lime juice
1 tbs. grated orange peel (zest)
1 tbs. grated lime peel (zest)
1/3 cup chopped fresh cilantro
pinch red pepper flakes
salt to taste
1 large tomato, chopped
1 can (6 oz.) crabmeat, drained
dash hot pepper sauce
4 large flour tortillas
vegetable spray
sliced avocado for garnish
lime wedges for garnish

In a medium bowl, combine Swiss cheese, cream cheese, citrus juices and zests, cilantro, red pepper flakes and salt. Mix well and set aside. In a smaller bowl, mix tomato, crab and hot pepper sauce; set aside. Coat a large skillet with vegetable spray. Place 1 tortilla in pan. Spread 1/2 of the cheese mixture over tortilla and top with 1/2 of the tomato-crab mixture. Press second tortilla over fillings to seal. Over medium-low heat, cook quesadillas until brown underneath. Carefully flip over and cook until underside is brown. Slide onto a serving dish. Repeat with remaining 2 tortillas and remaining fillings. Cut each quesadilla into 4 triangles. Garnish with sliced avocado and lime wedges.

BROILED VEGETABLE PANINI

Servings: 4

Panini means "little breads" in Italian and they are versatile luncheon appetizers. Simple to make and easy to eat, their popularity is understandable. Here, assorted vegetables are quickly broiled, tossed with fresh herbs and sandwiched between soft foccacia rolls.

8 cups diagonally cut assorted vegetables (eggplant, mushrooms, tomatoes, peppers and/or squash), 3/4-inch pieces
2 tbs. olive oil
3 cloves garlic, minced
2 tbs. chopped fresh basil
4 large foccacia rolls
4 large red or green lettuce leaves, stalk ends removed
salt and pepper to taste
1 cup crumbled feta cheese

Heat broiler. On a foil-covered baking sheet, mix vegetables with olive oil. Arrange one layer deep and broil for about 5 or 7 minutes, turning once, until cooked. Toss with basil and divide among lettuce-lined rolls. Add salt, pepper and feta cheese. Serve immediately.

GRILLED CHICKEN AND OLIVE PANINI

Servings: 4

Panini, small Italian open-faced sandwiches, make a brilliant light supper when appetites are not at their all-time high. A crisp white wine and assorted fruit are all that are needed to accompany this dish.

½ cup kalamata olive tapenade
2 tbs. extra virgin olive oil
1 round herbed foccacia, split horizontally
2 grilled chicken breast halves, thinly sliced
2 cups thinly sliced Roma tomatoes
½ lb. mozzarella cheese, sliced
1 cup basil leaves

Thin olive tapenade with olive oil. Spread foccacia bread with ½ of the olive tapenade mixture. Arrange chicken, tomatoes, mozzarella and basil leaves on bread. Top with the remaining tapenade. Serve or wrap with plastic film and refrigerate until serving.

GRILLED CHICKEN-STUFFED PITAS

Servings: 4

Leftover grilled chicken takes on Middle Eastern flavors for a lunch or dinner entrée. Fresh hummus, a paste made with ground garbanzo beans, comes in plastic tubs and is usually available in the refrigerated sections of food stores. For variety, substitute roasted lamb or grilled steak for the chicken.

2 cups finely chopped grilled chicken
1 cup finely chopped red onion
¼ cup fresh flat-leaf parsley
1 pkg. (7 oz.) hummus
2 tsp. ground cumin
salt and pepper to taste
1 cup chopped cucumber, peeled, seeded
1 cup chopped tomatoes
1 tbs. extra virgin olive oil

In a medium bowl, mix chicken, onion, parsley, hummus, cumin, salt and pepper. In another bowl, mix cucumber, tomatoes and olive oil. Cut pitas crosswise in half. Divide chicken mixture among 8 pita halves. Top each with 2 tbs. vegetable mixture. Wrap stuffed pitas tightly in wax paper, twisting ends to secure. Microwave in two batches on MEDIUM for 30 seconds until warm. Serve immediately.

CRUNCHY VEGETABLE BURRITOS

Servings: 4

This is a quick lunch that children will love. The older kids can assist shredding and chopping the vegetables and the younger ones can do all of the mixing. Everyone can help fill, wrap and enjoy them.

1 cup shredded carrots
1 cup chopped tender broccoli stems and florets
1 cup chopped tender cauliflower stems and florets
2 green onions, thinly sliced
½ cup raisins
½ cup sunflower seeds
½ lb. shredded reduced-fat cheddar cheese
½ tsp. chili powder
¼ cup nonfat ranch-style salad dressing
six 7-inch flour tortillas
2 cups shredded iceberg lettuce

In a large bowl, combine carrots, broccoli, cauliflower, onions, raisins and sunflower seeds with cheese, chili powder and dressing; mix well. Lay tortillas flat on the counter. Divide vegetable mixture, placing equal amounts in centers of tortillas. Top with lettuce. Fold one end of each tortilla up about 1 inch over filling. Fold right and left sides over folded end, so flaps overlap. Serve on plates and eat out of hand.

MARINATED STEAK SANDWICHES

Servings: 4

Steak sandwiches take on an Asian accent when prepared with teriyaki seasoning. Ginger adds zing and peanuts add crunch. Serve with finger-sized raw vegetables, green tea and coconut cookies for dessert.

½ cup plus 2 tbs. peanut oil
1 cup teriyaki sauce
1 clove garlic, minced
1 tsp. minced fresh ginger
¾ lb. boneless top-sirloin steak, cut into 1-inch-thick slices
4 large, soft steak rolls, cut in half horizontally
mixed baby greens
8 oz. fresh mozzarella cheese, sliced
1½ cups sliced shiitake mushrooms
½ cup thinly sliced green bell pepper
½ cup thinly sliced red bell pepper
½ cup thinly sliced red onion
1 cup finely chopped dry-roasted peanuts

In a large plastic freezer bag, combine 1/4 cup of the oil, teriyaki sauce, garlic and ginger; mix well. Add meat and marinate in the refrigerator for 10 to 14 hours, turning occasionally.

Heat broiler to 500°. Remove meat from marinade and wipe dry. Strain marinade and reserve. Place steak on broiler rack and broil 4 inches from heat to desired doneness. Carve steak against the grain into thin slices. On 4 large platters, arrange greens, steak and cheese over both halves of roll, open-face style; set aside. In a small skillet, add remaining 2 tbs. olive oil over high heat. Add mushrooms, pepper and onion slices. Stir-fry until tender-crisp, for about 2 minutes. Add reserved marinade and cook until bubbly. Pour mixture over sandwich, top with peanuts and serve.

QUICK TOMATO PIZZA

Servings: 4

An uncooked puttanesca sauce, an Italian tomato sauce mixed with anchovies, capers and black olives, tops these supermarket pizza shells for a quick, satisfying supper. Be sure to drain the tomatoes well before putting them on the pizza shells.

- 4 cups diced fresh tomatoes, well drained
- 2 cloves garlic, minced
- 6 anchovy fillets, drained and mashed
- 1 cup pitted Sicilian black olives, chopped
- 2 tbs. capers, rinsed and chopped
- 1/4 tsp. red pepper flakes
- two 12-inch pizza shells
- grated pecorino Romano cheese

Heat oven to 450°. In a large ceramic bowl, combine tomatoes, garlic, anchovies, olives, capers and red pepper flakes. Carefully spread mixture over both pizza shells. Sprinkle with cheese and bake for about 10 to 12 minutes until edges turn golden brown in color.

RAVIOLI PRIMAVERA

Servings: 4

One trip to the market is all you'll need to find the makings of this quick dinner. Cheese ravioli, pesto sauce, presliced vegetables and Parmesan cheese are the winning combination. Change the vegetables and cheese for variety. Try grated pecorino Romano cheese with packaged Italian-style veggies or creamy fontina cheese with a medley of lightly steamed fresh seasonal vegetables.

2 pkg. (10 oz. each) cheese-filled ravioli
4 qt. cold water
1 tsp. salt
2 pkg. (7 oz. each) frozen California-style mixed vegetables
1 cup prepared pesto sauce
1 cup grated Parmesan cheese

Cook ravioli according to package directions. Drain and place in a large, warm bowl. In an 8-quart saucepan, bring water to a boil. Add salt and frozen vegetables. Boil vegetables for 1 minute, or until tender-crisp; drain. Add vegetables to ravioli and toss with pesto sauce and 1/2 of the cheese. Pass remaining cheese at the table.

MACARONI AND PEAS

Servings: 2

One of the easiest, most economical dishes imaginable, this lunch is ready in minutes – thanks to the microwave oven.

1 cup tiny shell macaroni
1 small onion, finely chopped
1/4 cup extra virgin olive oil
2 cups frozen peas
salt and pepper to taste
freshly grated Romano cheese

Cook macaroni in a large pot of rapidly boiling salted water until slightly firm to the bite, or *al dente*, about 3 minutes. Drain pasta, reserving 1 cup of the water and leaving a little water clinging to the macaroni. Place in a warm bowl and keep warm.

In a 4-quart microwaveable bowl, cook onion in oil on HIGH for 10 minutes until soft and translucent. Add peas to onion mixture. Microwave on HIGH for 2 minutes to heat through. Fold in reserved macaroni, adding reserved macaroni water as needed. Season with salt, pepper and Romano cheese.

PASTA WITH SPICY TOMATO SHRIMP

Servings: 4

Fully-cooked baby shrimp star in this quick, spicy pasta dinner.

1 lb. linguini
2 tbs. extra virgin olive oil
1 tsp. red pepper flakes
1 jar (28 oz.) roasted garlic tomato sauce
1/2 cup clam juice
1 tsp. grated lemon peel (zest)
1 lb. cooked baby shrimp
asparagus tips for garnish, optional
sliced mushrooms for garnish, optional

Cook linguini in a large pot of rapidly boiling salted water until slightly firm to the bite, *al dente,* about 3 minutes. Drain pasta, reserving 1 cup of the warm water and leaving a little water clinging to the linguini. Place in a warm bowl and keep warm.

In a large skillet over medium-high heat, heat olive oil. Quickly stir-fry red pepper flakes until fragrant. Add tomato sauce, clam juice, lemon peel and shrimp. Bring to a boil. Lower heat and simmer for 5 minutes to allow flavors to blend, adding reserved linguini water if needed. Pour sauce over linguini. Serve as is or garnish with asparagus tips and mushrooms.

CHICKEN AND OLIVE PASTA

Servings: 4

In the tradition of country cooking, this outstanding chicken and olive sauté projects an earthy peasant taste, with its lusty use of red pepper flakes, olive oil, garlic and onions. A bit of refinement, however, from the use of butter, smooths the edges and makes the dish memorable.

1/4 cup olive oil
1/4 cup butter
1/2 cup chopped garlic
1 medium-sized yellow onion, chopped
1 tsp. red pepper flakes
1 tbs. dried oregano
1 1/2 lb. cooked chicken meat, cut into bite-sized pieces
18 green brine-cured olives, cracked with mallet or heavy knife
salt and pepper to taste
1/2 cup freshly grated pecorino Romano cheese
1 lb. rotelli or fussili pasta, cooked and kept warm

In a large skillet over medium-high heat, combine oil and butter. Add garlic and onion and cook for about 10 minutes, stirring occasionally, until garlic is brown and crunchy. Stir in red pepper, oregano, chicken and olives. Cook until heated through and adjust seasonings. Add cooked rotelli to pan and stir to blend. Serve in warm bowls with grated cheese.

Servings: 4

VARIATION: CHICKEN AND CAPER PASTA

Add 3 tbs. chopped lemon zest, 1½ tbs. rinsed capers and 1 cup dry white wine to the chicken-olive combination. Cook until wine has reduced to about ¼ cup. Proceed with recipe, but swirl additional butter into sauce before adding pasta.

PASTA WITH ZUCCHINI AND NECTARINES

Servings: 4

As most gardeners know, zucchini grows without boundaries, and new recipes utilizing the sprightly vegetable are always welcome. This innovative recipe shows off the best of the summer harvest. Sweet nectarines are welcome bites between mouthfuls of pasta shells and shreds of zucchini.

1 lb. medium sea shell pasta or ridged penne pasta
1/4 cup extra virgin olive oil
4 cloves garlic, minced
1 lb. zucchini, cut into 1/4-inch slices
1 cup minced fresh herbs, such as oregano, marjoram, thyme and parsley
salt and pepper to taste
1/2 cup grated Romano cheese
3 large nectarines, cut into 1/4-inch wedges

Cook shell pasta in a large pot of rapidly boiling salted water until slightly firm to the bite, or *al dente*, about 4 minutes. Drain shells, reserving ½ cup of the water and leaving a little water clinging to the macaroni. Place in a warm bowl and keep warm.

In a large skillet, heat olive oil over high heat. Sauté garlic, stirring frequently until golden. Reduce heat to medium. Add zucchini and herbs. Sauté for 8 to 10 minutes, until brown. Pour in ½ cup reserved pasta water, salt, pepper and cheese. Stir until creamy and mixture coats the back of a spoon. Fold in pasta shells and nectarine slices, and serve in warm dishes.

RICE SALAD WITH SHRIMP

Servings: 4

Make this in the morning for a quick, cool lunch on those torrid midsummer days. Cooking rice in shrimp bouillon, instead of water intensifies the shrimp flavor, providing a rich, smooth base for the rather assertive flavors of the other ingredients. Armenian cracker bread, minted iced tea, fruit and sugar cookies complete the meal.

2 cloves garlic, minced
3 tbs. lemon juice
2 tbs. chopped fresh basil leaves
salt and pepper to taste
1/4 tsp. red pepper flakes
1/2 cup extra virgin olive oil
1/2 lb. cooked baby shrimp
2 1/2 cups boiling water
2 shrimp bouillon cubes
2 cups instant rice
1 jar (10 oz.) roasted bell peppers, drained and chopped
1/2 cup pitted brine-cured green olives
1/2 cup pitted oil-cured black olives
1/4 cup chopped green onions

In a heavy-duty plastic bag, combine garlic, lemon juice, basil, salt, pepper, red pepper flakes and olive oil. Mix well and add shrimp to marinade. Refrigerate for 30 minutes, or up to 60 minutes, turning bag at least once.

Dissolve shrimp bouillon cubes in boiling water. Following package directions, cook instant rice in shrimp bouillon. When cool, place cooked rice in a large serving bowl. Fold peppers, olives, green onions and shrimp into rice. Mix well and chill for several hours. Divide salad among dinner plates and serve.

RICE NOODLES WITH TOFU PEANUT SAUCE

Servings: 4

Thai influence is evident in this easy-to-prepare vegetarian dinner.

½ lb. rice vermicelli noodles
⅓ cup crunchy peanut butter
1 can (7.5 oz.) coconut milk
3 cloves garlic, minced
2 tbs. soy sauce
2 tbs. white wine vinegar
¼ tsp. cayenne pepper
1 tsp. minced fresh ginger, or ¼ tsp. dried
2 tbs. peanut oil
2 cups thinly sliced cabbage
2 cups thinly sliced spinach
½ cup sliced green onions
2 cups bean sprouts
1 pkg. (14 oz.) firm tofu, cut into ½-inch cubes
1 cup fresh cilantro leaves
½ cup chopped dry-roasted peanuts

Cook rice vermicelli in rapidly boiling water stirring constantly, for 3 minutes until tender. Drain and rinse with hot water. Drain again and place in a warm bowl; keep warm.

In a small saucepan, combine peanut butter, coconut milk, garlic, soy sauce and white vinegar. Mix well and cook over medium heat for 3 minutes, or until well blended. Add cayenne pepper and ginger; set aside. Heat oil in a large skillet or wok. Over medium heat, stir-fry cabbage and spinach for 2 minutes, until wilted. Stir in onions, bean sprouts, tofu and peanut sauce. Bring to a boil. Cover and remove from heat. Divide vermicelli and greens mixture among 4 plates. Top with cilantro and dry-roasted peanuts. Serve immediately.

GARLIC AND GINGER SHRIMP

Servings: 4

When jumbo shrimp are available, prepare this simple pasta dinner and wait for the compliments. Garlic, ginger, basil and olive oil lend a Pacific Rim touch to these flavorful crustaceans. Complete the meal with a basic green salad, but splurge with something special for dessert.

12 uncooked jumbo shrimp, about 2 lb.
1 lb. linguini
4 large cloves garlic, minced
1 tbs. minced fresh ginger
1 tbs. chopped fresh lemon peel (zest)
1 cup chopped fresh basil leaves
½ tsp. red pepper flakes
1 tsp. salt
¾ cup extra virgin olive oil

Remove shells and dark veins from shrimp; set aside. In a heavy-duty plastic bag, combine garlic, ginger, lemon, basil, pepper, salt and olive oil. Mix well and add shrimp to marinade. Refrigerate for 30 minutes, or up to 60 minutes, turning bag at least once. Heat broiler.

Line a shallow baking pan with foil. Place drained shrimp over a wire rack over pan. Broil 4 inches from heat for 6 minutes.

Cook linguini in a large pot of rapidly boiling salted water until slightly firm to the bite, *al dente*, about 3 minutes. Drain pasta, leaving a little water clinging to it, and place in a warm bowl. Toss linguini with shrimp pan drippings. Arrange a nest of linguini on each plate, top each with 3 shrimp and serve.

SEA BASS WITH CITRUS

Servings: 4

Sea bass is moist, tender meat when baked quickly. Chilean sea bass, in particular, works well in this dish. Serve simply on top of white rice on a bed of microwaved collard, escarole or mild Chinese greens.

6 sea bass fillets, about 5 oz. each
1/4 cup mixed orange, lemon and lime juices
2 tbs. vegetable oil
salt and pepper to taste
1/4 cup chopped fresh oregano leaves
3 tbs. nonfat condensed milk
1 cup low-fat mayonnaise
24 Alfonso or kalamata olives, pitted and sliced
3 tbs. chopped fresh flat-leaf parsley
4 cups hot cooked rice
hot cooked collard greens, escarole or Chinese greens

Heat oven to 450°. Rub fillets with juice, oil, salt and pepper. Sprinkle with oregano. Bake on an oiled foil-lined baking sheet for 15 minutes, or until fish flakes easily when tested with a fork. Combine milk with mayonnaise, olives and parsley. Place fish on warm plates over rice and collards. Top with mayonnaise mixture.

CHINESE BROCCOLI (CHOY SUM) WITH SOY BEANS

Servings: 4

Exciting vegetables turn up at local farmers' markets nationwide. The leafy green ones cook quickly and make delicious lunches or light suppers. Try them steamed or microwaved, combined with various beans or rice and dressed with flavored oils or condiments.

2¼ cups instant brown rice
2 bunches (8 cups) Chinese broccoli leaves and tender stems, cut diagonally
1 cup frozen podded soy beans, thawed
1 tsp. garlic powder
4 tbs. hoisin sauce
1 cup chopped salted peanuts

Prepare brown rice according to package directions and keep warm. Steam or microwave greens and beans until tender-crisp; drain. Mix with garlic powder and hoisin. Serve on a bed of rice and top with peanuts.

THAI-STYLE BEEF

Servings: 4

This Asian stir fry makes a complete meal. Fish sauce (nam pla) and plum sauce are available at Asian markets.

- 1 lb. ground beef chuck
- 4-5 cups shredded green cabbage
- 3 green onions, finely chopped
- 2 jalapeño peppers, stemmed, seeded and minced
- 1 tbs. minced fresh ginger
- 3 tbs. fresh lime juice
- ½ tsp. salt
- 1 tsp. sugar
- 2 tsp. soy sauce
- 1½ tbs. fish sauce (nam pla)
- ½ cup chopped fresh cilantro, plus additional leaves for garnish
- ⅓ cup finely chopped unsalted dry-roasted peanuts
- eight 10-inch flour tortillas
- plum sauce, optional

Heat broiler. On a foil-lined baking sheet, combine beef, cabbage, onions, peppers, ginger, lime juice, salt, sugar, soy, fish sauce, cilantro and peanuts. Mix well and spread out on a sheet. Broil 6 inches from heat for 5 minutes. Turn ingredients over and broil for about 4 minutes until beef is no longer pink and cabbage is tender-crisp. Remove from oven and keep warm. Heat tortillas in microwave according to package directions. Divide beef mixture among tortillas and serve with plum sauce, if desired.

INDEX

Serve creative, easy, nutritious meals with nitty gritty® cookbooks